The Funniest People in Dance 250 Anecdotes

David Bruce

Published by David Bruce, 2022.

While every precaution has been taken in the preparation of this book, the publisher assumes no responsibility for errors or omissions, or for damages resulting from the use of the information contained herein.

THE FUNNIEST PEOPLE IN DANCE 250 ANECDOTES

First edition. September 3, 2022.

Copyright © 2022 David Bruce.

ISBN: 979-8215365755

Written by David Bruce.

Table of Contents

Dedication

Dedicated to My Brother Frank

Frank was reluctant to write the words below, but he did at my request because it's an opportunity to show that people still do good deeds. This can help restore people's faith in humanity.

"I've put some thought into this, and here a few Good Deeds I've done.

"I've bought breakfast more than once for complete strangers at my favorite local diner (Tommy's Diner) just because they looked like they could use a free meal.

"A woman came into Tommy's Diner, looking like she could use a decent meal and would appreciate it being free. I watched as she walked through the restaurant and sat down. I thought to myself, 'Buy her lunch.' I fought the urge and told myself no. I looked at her after she ordered and received her meal and thought to myself, 'Buy her lunch.' Again, I told myself no. She is a complete stranger, and money is hard to come by for me as well as everyone else. I was in line at the check-out waiting to pay my bill. She came up and got into line behind me and I thought to myself, 'Buy her lunch!' I looked at her, she looked at me, I reached out and grabbed her ticket, but she didn't want to let go. I told her sort of sternly, 'I don't know why, but I really, really want to pay for your lunch. I know we are complete strangers, but I feel like I am supposed to pay for your lunch. Will you please give me the pleasure of paying for this?' She almost cried, but she did allow me the pleasure.

"In Columbus, Ohio, almost always someone is at the gas station wanting money. One day this guy asked for money. I asked him, 'Why do you want money?' He said he's hungry. (If you don't know, Speedway has hotdogs and other food and drink items.) I said, 'Come inside, I'll buy you something to eat.' He was a really nice guy. His name was Dave, and he was an Army veteran; he may have been a little mentally ill after serving in the military. He talked to me about the war (don't know what war) and how he was over there fighting bulldozers. I think a couple of hotdogs and a hot coffee made his day. It really put a smile on his face. I ended up liking this guy and I'd look for him when I was getting gas so I could help him out.

"One time a guy came in the restaurant selling an old leather jacket for $10.00 so he could get some gas. It didn't fit me, and I didn't want it anyway, but I bought it and then donated the jacket.

"A woman was driving her car with the alarm going off, so I helped her figure out how to turn it off. She had the key fob, so I'm sure she didn't steal the car.

"These are a few of the good deeds I've had the pleasure of doing."

***

The doing of good deeds is important. As a free person, you can choose to live your life as a good person or as a bad person. To be a good person, do good deeds. To be a bad person, do bad deeds. If you do good deeds, you will become good. If you do bad deeds, you will become bad. To become the person you want to be, act as if you already are that kind of person. Each of us chooses what kind of person we will become. To become a good person, do the things a good person does. To become a bad person, do the things a bad person does. The opportunity to take action to become the kind of person you want to be is yours.

Cover Photograph for *The Funniest People in Dance*:

Photographer: Anestiev

https://pixabay.com/photos/girl-jump-happy-dance-sea-beach-6096180/

All anecdotes have been retold in my own words to avoid plagiarism.

Anecdotes are usually short humorous stories. Sometimes they are thought-provoking or informative, not amusing.

Do you know a language other than English? If you do, I give you permission to translate this book, copyright your translation, publish or self-publish it, and keep all the royalties for yourself. (Do give me credit, of course, for the original book.)

Chapter 1: From Activism to Christmas

Activism

• In some South American countries, people who are critical of the government disappear — agents of the government kidnap and kill them. Some relatives and friends of the *desapariciones* have attracted international attention to the problem by unusual protests — going on hunger strikes, sewing quilts, and dancing alone to show that they miss the disappeared.[1]

• African-American choreographer Alvin Ailey, Jr., created *Masekela Langage* to protest apartheid in South Africa. In the dance's climax, a bloodied black man staggers into a party and dies. The program note for *Masekela Langage* states, "Looks like it's safer to be in jail."[2]

Animals

• Ballerina Alice Patelson's mother was a former Radio City Rockette who taught ballet to neighborhood children in a studio built into her home. Whenever Alice's mother came downstairs dressed in her leotard to begin teaching a ballet class, the family pet springer spaniel, Lady, went upstairs. When Lady thought the family was busy, she would take a flying leap into the middle of Alice's parents' bed, which was forbidden to her. However, the family knew what Lady was doing. After ballet class was over, Alice's mother used to noisily climb upstairs, giving Lady plenty of warning to get off the bed before being caught.[3]

• In her act, belly dancer Amaya — née Maria Elena Amaya — used a snake that ate three mice a month. Unfortunately, one month the local pet shop ran out of mice, so the pet shop owner suggested, "Three mice = six baby chicks." However, Amaya remembered what had happened when a belly dancer friend had fed her snake baby chicks. At the conclusion of a dance in Las Vegas, the belly dancer had lifted the snake over her head, and the snake had loudly passed gas. Not only did the snake emit gas, but it also emitted a cloud of baby chick feathers.[4]

• When Rudolf Nureyev was a young child growing up in Ufa, food was scarce and he was frequently hungry. One day, his mother made a long trek through the snow to another village in search of food to feed her family at home. Near nightfall, she noticed yellowish circles of light around her — circles of light that traveled in pairs. Suddenly, she realized that wolves had surrounded her. She took off the blanket she was wearing around her shoulders and set it on fire. Seeing the fire, the wolves fled.[5]

• While studying black dance in Haiti, Katherine Dunham was invited to stay at the home of a friend. However, she smelled something unusual in the house and looked up to see an 8-foot python in the rafters. The snake was a "pet" often kept around Haitian homes to eat rats and mice.[6]

Arguments

• Early in her career, Martha Graham was a dancer for Denishawn. Both she and Denishawn co-founder Ted Shawn had tempers. One day, while on tour, Ms. Graham called Mr. Shawn to say that she wanted to add a new dance to the tour. Mr. Shawn refused to give her permission to add the dance, so Ms. Graham angrily ripped the telephone out of the wall. On another occasion, they grew angry as they talked over lunch in a New York restaurant. Ms. Graham stood up, grabbed the tablecloth, and pulled it, the dishes, and all the food onto the floor, and then she stalked out of the restaurant and into a taxi. Mr. Shawn followed her and screamed at her, "I don't ever want to see you again in my life! And I mean it!" On both occasions, they quickly made up their differences.[7]

• When Lindy Hop dancer Norma Miller was underage, she had a chance to go to Europe as a member of a dance troupe. The problem was this: How could she convince her mother to let her go? After receiving the offer, she went home and her mother, who was tired, asked her to do a favor — to wash a few things in the sink. Norma asked, "Okay, Ma, but if I wash out your underwear, will you let me go to Europe?" Thinking that Norma was joking, her mother said, "Yes, if you wash those things in the sink, I'll let you go to Europe." The next day Norma told her about the offer — and reminded her about her promise to let her go to Europe. After a lot of arguing, and the promise that Norma would be chaperoned, her mother let her go to Europe.[8]

Audiences

• Agnes de Mille said, "I'm not a Massine fan at all." When Léonide Massine was at Covent Garden, his fans were numerous and enthusiastic. Ms. de Mille used to attend performances of his works at Covent Garden and be very quiet. Meanwhile, members of the audience would cheer madly, be wildly extravagant in their love for Massine and his art — and glare at Ms. de Mille because she did not share their enthusiasm for all things Massine. One day, Mr. Massine was introduced at Covent Garden as "certainly the greatest choreographer we have living and probably ever have had." Ms. de Mille immediately thought of Martha Graham and of Antony Tudor.[9]

• Anita Berber, known mainly as a controversial dancer in Weimar Berlin, performed in many countries. In Fiume, a city now in Croatia, she performed in a very small club where she could hear the comments members of the audience made about her. She overheard one insulting comment and memorized where it had come from. After her dance was over, she walked over to that spot and slapped the man sitting there. Unfortunately, Ms. Berber was nearsighted and did not know that the man who had insulted her had gone and that a man who appreciated her talent had taken his place.[10]

• Being a nonconformist sometimes leads to opportunities. In London early in her career, modern dance pioneer Isadora Duncan and Raymond, her brother, danced in the park. Enjoying their impromptu performance was a woman who invited them to her home, where Isadora again danced. The woman was the famous actress Mrs. Patrick

Campbell, who introduced Isadora and her brother to other famous and wealthy people, and soon Isadora was performing in their homes. [11]

• In 1976, Twyla Tharp created a piece for herself and Mikhail Baryshnikov. The piece contained no virtuoso acrobatic dance moves, and Mr. Baryshnikov did not leave the ground at all during the dance. The two danced the piece at a gala at the Metropolitan Opera House, and the audience — which wanted virtuoso acrobatic dance moves — booed them. Mr. Baryshnikov had never been booed before — and all the boos delighted him.[12]

• Vaslav Nijinsky's *Le Sacre du Printemps* caused a furor when it was first performed. At first, audiences hated it, and they made much noise during its presentation, once causing impresario Sergei Diaghilev to shout at the audience, "Silence! The dancers cannot hear the music!" Later, audiences appreciated the ballet.[13]

• What a ballerina remembers about a performance may not be what the audience remembers. Early in her career, Violette Verdy danced the role of Cinderella at La Scala. What she remembers most about the production is something about the audience: the gleaming of men's bald heads in the dim light.[14]

• In 1907, Isadora Duncan danced in Moscow. At the end of the first act, some audience members hissed because of their lack of appreciation for her art, but Constantine Stanislavsky, the co-director of the Moscow Art Theater, stood up and applauded vigorously. Recognizing him, the hissers stopped.[15]

• Whenever the Merce Cunningham Dance Company performed, many dancers sat in the audience. A non-dancer at a performance looked at the audience members as they walked around during the intermission and said, "I've never seen an audience so erect, with such beautiful posture."[16]

Auditions

• Mary Anthony danced so impressively at an audition that Hanya Holm gave her a three-year tuition waiver. Ms. Anthony believed that she was successful at the audition because she owned only one record. She was required to dance two solos, and after she had danced to the music of the one record she owned, she danced her second solo without music. This "decision" of hers so impressed Ms. Holm that she gave her the tuition waiver.[17]

• When ballet impresario Sergei Diaghilev asked Russian ballerina Alexandra Danilova to audition for him, she was indignant and told him, "Do you know that I am from the Mariinsky Theater? If I am good enough for the Mariinsky Theater, I am good enough for you!" She auditioned anyway, but she was further insulted when Mr. Diaghilev asked her about her weight. She stormed, "Are you buying a horse? Maybe you want to see my teeth!"[18]

Autographs

• In June of 1952, Le Grand Ballet du Marquis de Cuevas danced in Rio de Janeiro. Some ballet fans went backstage, where they quickly stole as many small souvenirs as possible, including many, many photographs that George Zoritch kept of himself in his dressing room. These fans brought the photographs around to Mr. Zoritch, who of course recognized where they had come from, but who signed them anyway. Soon, Mr. Zoritch noticed that the same people kept asking him to sign his photograph. He pointed out that he had already given them an autograph, but they said, "Yes, we already have two or three, but would you autograph one more?"[19]

• George Balanchine took the New York City Ballet on a tour to his native Russia and throughout Europe, ending the tour in Poland. During the tour, the ballet company carried grey linoleum flooring to dance on. In Poland, Mr. Balanchine made a present of the flooring to the Polish Ballet School after autographing a corner of it. An official of the Polish Ballet School cut off the corner that Mr. Balanchine had autographed, and then he framed it and hung it up.[20]

• As a young girl, ballerina Illaria Obidenna Ladré had a crush on Russian dancer Anatole Vilzak. She met him after she graduated from dance school, and he wrote two lines in her yearbook — "First of all love / dance and art" — and signed his name. Illaria crossed out the line "dance and art," leaving "First of all love."[21]

• A man once saw dancer/choreographer Martha Graham surrounded by fans, so he asked her for her autograph, which she gave to him. But after reading the name on the piece of paper, he asked, "Who are you?" Ms. Graham grabbed the piece of paper from his hand and then snapped, "Find out!"[22]

• Famous mime Marcel Marceau once watched ballet dancer Peter Martins rehearse and was so impressed that he autographed Mr. Martins' arm and added his impression of Mr. Martins' talent: "Wonderful!" [23]

Censorship

• Dance can be censored. The Danny Grossman Dance Company performed *National Spirit* — a dance that satirizes American patriotism and implies that blindly following your leader can get you killed — at a Florida elementary school. The company was supposed to perform two shows, but after the first performance, the principal would not allow them to perform the second. She told Mr. Grossman, "It will take ten years to unteach what you have shown them." She also called the police to escort the dance troupe out of the school.[24]

• Anna Pavlova was once censored while dancing in the United States. The authorities thought that the skirts of her ballet costumes were too short, so they made her wear longer skirts before allowing her to perform. About this experience, Ms. Pavlova said, "The evil was in the mind of my critics, I think, rather than in the beautiful art which it has always been my endeavor to give to the world."[25]

• In Romania in the mid-1940s, censors sometimes read people's mail. Ballerina Illaria Obidenna Ladré lived in Romania for a while as her husband, Marian Ladré, danced in South America. He once sent her a photograph of himself, and the censor wrote underneath the photograph, "What a handsome husband you have!"[26]

Children

• When ballerina Margot Fonteyn was a little girl, her mother knew how to keep her quiet, at least for a short time. She would put a pin on the floor, put a cushion on the pin, then have little Margot sit on the cushion. She would tell little Margot that if she sat quietly, fairies would turn the pin into a lump of sugar. However, little Margot was not allowed to talk, and she was not allowed to look to see if the pin had turned into a lump of sugar, because if she did, the transformation of the pin into a lump of sugar would take longer. Her mother would then do whatever chore she needed to do, such as baking a cake. Once or twice, she would check on the pin, say it hadn't turned into a lump of sugar yet, then return to the chore. However, when the chore was finished, miraculously the pin would have turned into a lump of sugar. [27]

• Beth Joiner, a children's dance teacher in Georgia, plays along when her students decide a certain day is "Opposite Day." Unfortunately, she learns what day it is after a student comes in and tells her that she is really pretty. When she thanks the student, all of her students snicker and say, "It's Opposite Day." Miss Beth then tells everybody how terrible they are when they dance well and how graceful they are when they dance badly. However, Opposite Day does result in problems. Once, a student told Miss Beth that her hair looked terrible, and when Miss Beth cheerfully replied, "Thank you," the student looked confused. On another occasion, Miss Beth got into Opposite Day so much that she created a family crisis by telling her mother-in-law that she was growing fat.[28]

• Isadora Duncan's early life was harsh after her mother separated from her father. Little money was available, and the family was forced to move from dwelling to dwelling. When Ms. Duncan was nearly eight years old, her school class was asked to write a story about their lives. The other children wrote happy stories, but little Isadora wrote about unkind landlords. Her teacher thought she was making up lies, and so the teacher spoke to Isadora's mother about the story. Isadora's mother started crying and said that the story was true. (Despite the lack of money, Isadora was introduced to culture very early in her life. Her mother played classical music on the piano and read Shakespeare to her children.)[29]

• In the USSR, ballerinas were major celebrities — and in the countries formed by the breakup of the USSR, they are still major celebrities. A group of children from Moldavia was visiting the Bolshoi when they found out that Galina Ulanova was practicing in a room next door. The children raced around the adults trying to keep them out of the practice room and watched her, entranced. Such scenes are repeated. When Ms. Ulanova returned to Leningrad to dance as a guest, its citizens were excited. As she warmed up, a door to the balcony over her warming-up area opened and some children stood and watched her, spellbound.[30]

• As a child, Agnes de Mille saw Anna Pavlova dance twice. She was mesmerized each time and motivated to study dancing. The second time she saw Ms. Pavlova dance, she was able to visit her backstage with a few adult friends. Ms. Pavlova kissed her on the cheek and gave her some flowers, and Agnes was so overwhelmed at being in the star's presence that she began to cry. Years later, Agnes learned that Ms. Pavlova acted that way with all the little girls who were brought to see her. But it didn't matter to Agnes, for Ms. Pavlova was a star of dance. [31]

• After World War II, in which she worked for the Resistance and was awarded the *croix de guerre* and the Legion of Honor with the Rosette of the Resistance, Josephine Baker adopted 12 orphans of several nationalities (including Finland, Ivory Coast, Korea, and Algeria) and several religions (including Buddhist, Shinto, Catholic, Jewish, and Muslim) and brought them to live with her in France. She called the adopted orphans the Rainbow Tribe and hoped that they would be a model for world brotherhood.[32]

• Everyone — including creative, successful, famous people — has been rejected at one time or another. When she was a teenager, young people's author Jean Little attended a party where a chaperone encouraged her to participate in a Sadie Hawkins dance where her partner would be whoever was closest to her when a piece of music stopped. Unfortunately, the boy closest to her looked at her, said, "Oh, God, no" — then left her on the dance floor. (She spent the rest of the evening standing behind the record player.)[33]

• When children's book author/illustrator Tomie dePaola was growing up, he took dance lessons and occasionally participated in a dance concert with the other child dancers. One year, he was supposed to dance as a pirate, and he wanted to have an eye patch so he could look scary. Therefore, he started giving his dance teacher, Miss Leah, some drawings of pirates. Each pirate wore an eye patch. Miss Leah got the hint, and she allowed Tomie to wear an eye patch during the dance. [34]

• At age four, future Olympic gymnast Shannon Miller had a problem. Tessa, her older sister, was taking dance lessons, but money was tight and young Shannon could not take lessons with her sister. She solved the problem the next time her grandmother telephoned. Talking on the phone, young Shannon told her the sad story, and Grandma agreed to pay for her lessons.[35]

• As a very young dance student, Suzanne Farrell often practiced at home, using an armchair to represent a male partner. She had read about and liked the male dancer Jacques d'Amboise, so she named the armchair after him. Later, as a dancer with the New York City Ballet, Ms. Farrell danced with the real Jacques d'Amboise.[36]

• Even as a young boy, Rudolf Nureyev loved dancing. One of his report cards included a notation by a teacher who stated that young

Rudolf "jumps like a frog and that's about all he knows. He even dances on the staircase landings."[37]

• As a very young dance pupil — 14 years old — Margot Fonteyn (then known as Margaret Hookham) showed much ambition. When she was told that Ms. Anna Pavlova was the greatest dancer in the world, she replied, "Then I will be the second greatest."[38]

• When Anna Pavlova was eight years old, her mother took her for the first time to the ballet, saying, "You are going to see the country of the fairies." Her mother spoke truly — the ballet was Tchaikovsky's *Sleeping Beauty*.[39]

• When Elise, ballerina Maria Tallchief's daughter, was very young, she wrote a poem that began, "Because she is my mother, / every night she turns into Cinderella."[40]

Choreographing

• Felia Doubrovska taught at George Balanchine's School of American Ballet for 30 years, and before that she danced in many of his works. Mr. Balanchine, of course, often fell in love with muses, who inspired him to create some of his masterpieces for them. He also often made his muses either his wives or his girlfriends, and many of them — Tamara Geva, Alexandra Danilova, Vera Zorina, Maria Tallchief, and Tanaquil Le Clercq — became famous. Ms. Doubrovska remained simply friends with Mr. Balanchine, who told her, "Our relationship is so nice, the way we can look each other in the eyes. My girlfriends and wives I try to forget." Ms. Doubrovska half-joked that she was a "little sad" that she had not been one of his girlfriends or wives "because then I would be famous."[41]

• George Balanchine choreographed many ballets for the New York City Ballet. Other companies tried to perform his ballets, but they weren't as successful as his own company; however, this didn't bother Mr. Balanchine. He once explained that he loved to play the piano, although he played it badly. When he tried to play difficult compositions such as Brahms' Second Piano Concerto, he loved playing them, although he performed them badly. And so, Mr. Balanchine explained, "That's why I understand those other companies when they dance my ballets. They do them badly, but they love them. Let them enjoy themselves!"[42]

• Thommie Walsh is the dancer whose pose with crossed arms appeared in posters for *A Chorus Line.* According to Mr. Walsh, the pose came from being bored in rehearsals and waiting for choreographer Michael Bennett to create dances. However, after Mr. Walsh became a choreographer, he realized how horrible his body language had been, and he telephoned Mr. Bennett to apologize, saying, "I know now what it's like, with ten or twelve dancers standing around, waiting for me to come up with the steps, the idea, to move it, to shake it. I know what it must have been like with me standing there with my arms crossed."[43]

• Robert Gottlieb disliked John Cranko's *Eugene Onegin* in part because of what he called "its patched-together Tchaikovsky score" — so did George Balanchine. Mr. Cranko had died young of a heart attack, but Mr. Balanchine told Mr. Gottlieb that he had died because of a different reason: "Tchaikovsky up in heaven looked down and saw that ballet and went to God and said, 'Get that one!'" Of course, Mr. Balanchine was aware of his place in history as a great choreographer, and when someone once asked him his opinion of the other choreographers, he answered, "And *who* are the other choreographers?" [44]

• Sergei Diaghilev motivated his choreographers by telling them, "Astonish me!" They responded by astonishing the world. On May 19, 1912, when Vaslav Nijinsky's *Afternoon of a Faun (L'Après-Midi d'un Faune)* premiered, it was a seminal, groundbreaking event. At first, the audience did not know what to make of it, and some boos and catcalls were heard as the ballet ended. However, Mr. Diaghilev ordered the ballet to be encored, and this time when the ballet ended, the audience responded with a great ovation.[45]

• Vaslav Nijinsky choreographed his ballet titled *L'Après-Midi d'un Faune* to Debussy's music, which was a prelude to Mallarmé's poem. Mr. Nijinsky created much consternation for everyone at a dinner party, all of whom thought the ballet was a wonderful introduction to Mallarmé's poem, when he confessed that he had not read that poem by Mallarmé — or any poem by Mallarmé.[46]

• While the great choreographer George Balanchine was lying in a hospital bed dying, one of his former wives, Maria Tallchief, visited him. Music was playing, and Mr. Balanchine was tapping his fingers together. Ms. Tallchief asked, "What are you doing, George?" He replied, "You see, I'm making steps."[47]

• When dancer Georges Skibine decided to become a choreographer, he asked the great George Balanchine for advice. Mr. Balanchine said simply, "Listen to the music and wait." Mr. Skibine's goal for his dancers became "not to dance *to* music, but to dance *the* music."[48]

Christmas

• Alicia Markova was dancing the role of the Sugar Plum Fairy when Doris, her sister, sitting in the audience, overheard a little boy give what Ms. Markova considered the greatest compliment of her career. The little boy saw the Sugar Plum Fairy, then turned to his mother and said, "Can I have her for my Christmas tree next year?"[49]

Chapter 2: From Clothing to Fans

Clothing

• Belly dancer Amaya — née Maria Elena Amaya — well remembers her most enthusiastic audience ever. She owned her own dance studio, and at night she turned it into a club. For a performance one night, she decided to wear a red bra that fastened in the front, along with a gold vest. As she danced, the audience grew more and more enthusiastic, clapping and cheering. After the dance, she was called out for three encores. Finally, one of her belly-dancing students revealed the reason for the audience's enthusiasm. Her bra had become undone, but she hadn't noticed because she was concentrating on the dance and because her vest had kept pressure on her breasts. However, the audience had definitely noticed. Amaya's husband had been in the audience, cheering like everyone else — and taking photographs. She had the photographs developed, then looked at them in sequence. Early in the dance, she was showing a little cleavage, which grew greater and greater as her dance progressed. The final photograph showed that the dance had stopped just before she would have revealed all.[50]

• David Janssen, star of TV's *The Fugitive*, and dancer Fred Astaire went to the same tailor. One day, Mr. Janssen went into the tailor's shop and saw Mr. Astaire with a new suit. Mr. Astaire had rolled up the suit and was busy throwing it against the wall. When Mr. Janssen asked what he was doing, Mr. Astaire replied, "The way to wear clothes is to tell them who's boss in the beginning. Then they fit you."[51]

• While dancing in San Francisco, ballerina Alicia Markova needed new stockings. She entered a clothing store and told the saleslady her size, but the saleslady replied, "*Nobody* has feet that small!" However, Ms. Markova did, so the saleslady advised her to exercise more so her feet would grow bigger.[52]

Competition

• At the 1969 International Ballet Competition held in Moscow, Mikhail Baryshnikov danced the lead role in *Vestris*. Among the judges was famed ballerina Maya Plisetskaya, who was so impressed by the young dancer's ability that instead of giving him the maximum 12 points for his rating, she gave him 13 points. As you would expect, Mr. Baryshnikov won the gold medal for the competition.[53]

• At the 1966 International Ballet Competition held in Varna, Bulgaria, Canadian ballerina Martine Van Hamel won the overall prize for artistic interpretation as well as the women's prize for dancing. Ironically, at her last performance, as she was taking a bow, she slipped and fell.[54]

• In 1949, in Johannesburg, South Africa, Anton Dolin was introduced as "the greatest dancer in the world" to an African dancer, who immediately shouted, "No, *I* am."[55]

Costumes

• In addition to being an innovator in dance techniques, modern dance pioneer Martha Graham was a pioneer in costuming. In ballet, costumes reveal the legs; however, during Ms. Graham's period of long woolens, she wore long woolen dresses that she would manipulate with her legs and body to stretch and create dramatic shapes. She took pains with her costumes, and if they weren't right, she would tear them apart and work with them until they were right. Sometimes, her dancers would use safety pins to hold their costumes together because no time was left to sew them together again in a new pattern after Ms. Graham had ripped them to pieces.[56]

• Ballet companies, not dancers, usually own the ballet costumes — although the dancers do supply their own leotards. This means that more than one dancer wears the costumes. Alicia Markova insisted that her costumes be cleaned each time she was to wear them. At a performance of *Romeo and Juliet*, Nora Kaye came backstage to change into her next costume — but she discovered that that costume and the others had been taken to the cleaners by an overeager dresser who was following Ms. Markova's orders. No costume changes took place in that performance of *Romeo and Juliet*.[57]

• Modern dance pioneer Isadora Duncan was also a pioneer in dance costuming. She often wore little more than a short, filmy tunic and left her legs and arms bare. In fact, many women of the time wore more clothing while swimming than Ms. Duncan danced in. Early in her career, she danced for upper-class ladies at teas and garden parties. At least once, some ladies left during her performances because they were scandalized by her lack of clothing. Late in her career, evangelist Billy Sunday complained, "That Bolshevik hussy doesn't wear enough clothes to pad a crutch!"[58]

• Early in her dancing career, Martha Graham appeared in the *Greenwich Village Follies*, where she represented artistic dancing in a production otherwise filled with dancing chorus girls. Each day, a police officer arrived to look over the dancers' costumes to make sure that they didn't violate any public decency laws. One day, a dancer pointed to Ms. Graham and asked, "What about her?" Although Ms. Graham's costume was the skimpiest one there, the police officer shrugged and said, "She's all right — she's art."[59]

• Choreographer Bronislava Nijinska danced the part of the hostess in her ballet *Les Biches*. As she was blocking out the pattern of the dance onstage, she held a cigarette holder as she always did, despite the regulations against smoking backstage. Sergei Diaghilev saw her with the cigarette holder, then insisted that it become part of the costume for her character. Often, Ms. Nijinska drank a glass of champagne just before going onstage because it helped put her in the mood of the character.[60]

• In the musical *One Touch of Venus*, an ancient statue of the goddess of love comes to life. Nymphs are dancers in the play, and the costumer designed costumes that shocked choreographer Agnes de Mille, who pointed out, "There seem to be breasts under her arms and on her back, too." The costumer replied, "You wouldn't want ordinary anatomy on nymphs, surely!" (Fortunately, Ms. de Mille did want ordinary anatomy on the nymphs.)[61]

• Costumes need not be expensive. Ted Shawn and Ruth St. Denis once went into a Woolworth's, where they shocked the clerks by putting colanders on their heads and saying such things as, "Look, dear, this strainer fits perfectly." After they had purchased a colander, they painted it gold and silver, added fake jewels and other gewgaws, and suddenly the colander had turned into an exotic Oriental headdress.[62]

• Dance and dancers change over time. Alvin Ailey, Jr., has said that members of his original company would not have been able to dance his later works such as *Streams* or *Choral Dances*. In fact, one of his original dancers told him, "We couldn't have got into these leotards, never mind cope with the technical challenges."[63]

• Ballerina Yvette Chauviré always took rehearsals seriously, regarding them as important as the actual performance. Once, at a rehearsal of Tchaikovsky's *Sleeping Beauty* at Covent Garden, she was the only dancer in costume.[64]

Critics

• After Merce Cunningham and his dancers had performed at a matinee in London's Saville Theatre in 1966, Merce Cunningham dancer Carolyn Brown answered the questions of several students who came backstage. One student asked, "Is he serious? I mean, isn't he just pulling our leg?" Ms. Brown thought about her answer, then replied, "Do you really believe that a man would spend his whole life working this hard, even going into debt, merely to pull *your* leg?"[65]

• Louis Horst wrote a review in *Dance Observer* of a 1957 Paul Taylor Dance Company concert that did not contain even a single conventional dance step, instead featuring such things as a man and a woman sitting motionless beside each other as they listened to a composition by John Cage. At the top of the page containing the review appeared the name and the date of the concert. The rest of the page was blank, except for Mr. Horst's initials at the bottom of the page.[66]

• On May 1, 1965, Twyla Tharp danced in the first piece of music she had ever choreographed: "Tank Dive." The next morning she bought the major New York newspapers, eager to find out what the critics had thought of her performance and her choreography. Fortunately, she didn't find any bad reviews. Unfortunately, she didn't find *any* reviews. She said, "I couldn't believe the critics didn't realize what we had here was history created last night."[67]

Death

• Ballet dancers have extremely strong legs. In 1840, Fanny Elssler crossed the Atlantic on the very first steamship for passengers. One day, she discovered a jewel thief in her cabin. She was alone, and she was unarmed, so she used her ballet muscles and kicked the jewel thief — the ballet kick killed him.[68]

• African-American choreographer Alvin Ailey, Jr., created *Memoria* in memory of his friend Joyce Trisler. When Mr. Ailey died, Gary DeLoatch danced the lead role in *Memoria*, but this time the lead role was not the part of Joyce Trisler. Instead, the lead role was the part of Mr. Ailey.[69]

Education

• When Choo Chiat Goh, the father of Chan Hon Goh, was a young dancer in London, he had a chance to dance for Anton Dolin's company, but he turned it down because he wished to study dance in China under Pyotr Gusiev. Later, Mr. Goh opened a dance studio in Vancouver, Canada, where his daughter took classes from him. Hearing that Mr. Dolin was in Vancouver, Mr. Goh invited him to watch a dance class. Mr. Dolin accepted the offer, and after the class he pointed to a student and told Mr. Goh, "That one — she has it. Yes, she is going to be a beautiful dancer." Mr. Goh was not sure which dancer Mr. Dolin meant. It looked like he was pointing to his daughter, but to make sure, Mr. Goh called Chan Hon over and asked Mr. Dolin, "You are talking about her?" Mr. Dolin replied, "Yes," and Mr. Goh said, "She is my daughter." Mr. Dolin's prophecy was accurate. Chan Hon Goh became a beautiful dancer — and a prima ballerina for the National Ballet of Canada.[70]

• When Ruthanna Boris was a young dancer, she was second to Marie-Jeanne, who danced solos. One day, after complaining to her mother, she (and especially her mother) decided that she should ask choreographer George Balanchine for solos. She did, and she started crying. Mr. Balanchine told her, "Don't cry, and don't tell me what your mother wants. And don't ask me for solos." Then Mr. Balanchine, who Ms. Boris says spoke in parables, asked her, "Do you know how to make a Caesar salad?" For 30 minutes, he explained how to make a Caesar salad, starting with obtaining fresh ingredients. When he had finished instructing her, he said, "You see how long it takes and how much you have to know and how you have to work to make a Caesar salad?" He then said, "Now go away," and let her contemplate what the parable had to say about learning to dance.[71]

• Early in her career, while she was still a student at Denishawn, Martha Graham showed talent, but she had not yet made a major impression on Ted Shawn. One day, Mr. Shawn and some of his students were working on "Serenata Morisca," a solo Moorish gypsy dance, as Mr. Shawn tried to decide who would perform it during the next tour. At one point, he looked at Ms. Graham, who as usual was sitting quietly and observing when she was not dancing, and he said, "It's too bad Martha doesn't know this dance. She would look just right in it." Ms. Graham spoke up, "But I do know it." Mr. Shawn replied, "That's impossible — you've never danced it!" Ms. Graham then demonstrated the dance, which she had learned from watching the other dancers. She was given the solo to perform during the tour.[72]

• Arthur Mitchell of the Dance Theatre of Harlem used to go to schools for lecture demonstrations and say, "I don't go much to discothèques anymore, so you've got to tell me what the latest dances are. Anybody want to come up and show me?" Once the students were up on stage demonstrating the newest dances, Mr. Mitchell would point out when appropriate, "Now you may call this step the 'hustle' or the 'monkey' or whatever, but what you were really doing was step, *plié*, step, *plié*," and show the student what he meant. Occasionally, one of the students demonstrating the newest dance steps would have real talent, and Mr. Mitchell would give the student a dance scholarship. [73]

• Dance teacher Carmelita Maracci was gifted. She was technically perfect and would demonstrate a dance move such as an *arabesque* to her astonished students, then invite them to try it. They were unable to reach her level of perfection, but they did the move better than they ever had before. One day, dancer Anton Dolan visited her classroom, so she stood up and unleased a series of dance moves — *entrechats six* and *entrechats huit* — that he had not been able to do since he was 30 years old (and that very few male dancers, and even fewer female dancers, can do), and then she sat down. After Mr. Dolan left, Ms. Maracci said, "It nearly sprung me, but I figured I had to do it. He'd heard I was a technician."[74]

• Edward Villella worked three hard years to learn how to partner a ballerina — before he learned to partner, he sometimes found it difficult to get ballerinas to dance with him. However, eventually he learned partnering — and learned it well. At Jacob's Pillow, he partnered the wondrous ballerina Violette Verdy in the *Tchaikovsky Pas de Deux*, and she got off balance during a series of turns. Fortunately, Mr. Villella was ready to immediately balance her again. At the close of the adagio, when he was holding Ms. Verdy upside down and she was looking up at him, she said, "Thanks!" — in perfect tempo to the music.[75]

• As a young man, choreographer George Balanchine nearly died and so he believed in living his life each day and not holding anything back. He would tell his dancers, "Why are you stingy with yourselves? Why are you holding back? What are you saving for — for another time? There are no other times. There is only now. Right now." Throughout his career, including before he became world renowned, he worked with what he had, not complaining about wanting a bigger budget or better dancers. One of the pieces of advice Mr. Balanchine gave over and over was this: "Do it now."[76]

• Miss Beth and Miss Lynn, two children's dance teachers in Georgia, once figured out a way to communicate with each other that they thought their students four years old and younger would not understand — they spelled. So they would make comments about students such as "P-R-E-T-T-Y G-O-O-D," "B-A-D child," "S-C-A-R-E-D," and "S-M-A-R-T A-S-S." Unfortunately, one four-year-old genius told them, "P-R-E-T-T-Y G-O-O-D spells 'pretty good,' B-A-D spells 'bad,' S-C-A-R-E-D spells 'scared,' S-M-A-R — .'" Miss Beth and Miss Lynn stopped spelling.[77]

• When Patricia McBride was a young dancer in the New York City Ballet, taking a pointe class with Felia Doubrovska, she saw ballerina Violette Verdy blowing kisses in her direction. She looked behind herself to see to whom these marks of approval were intended, but no one was behind her, so she realized that Ms. Verde was showing her approval of the way that she — young Patricia — was dancing. Ms. McBride says, "This was a first and lasting impression of Violette: a picture of spontaneity, enthusiasm, and charm."[78]

• Anna Pavlova was interested in culture, and she wanted members of her dance company — many of them teenaged girls — to also be interested in culture. While the company was touring by train, Ms. Pavlova used to walk up and down the corridors to see what her dancers were reading. However, the dancers knew that she would be checking up on them, and knowing that she approved of the *Saturday Evening Post*, they would use this large magazine to hide what they were really reading: romance novels.[79]

• Some people can't see what is in front of them. A young dancer took a class with master choreographer George Balanchine, but she never listened to him. One day, she started to leave class in a great hurry at the end, and Mr. Balanchine asked her why she was in such a hurry to leave. The young dancer explained that she was going to take another class with a Balanchine expert. This shocked and amused Mr. Balanchine. He told the dancer, "Here I am. It's me. I'm Balanchine. Why go anywhere else?"[80]

• Even an elderly ballerina can remain in control of parts of her art. In 1959, while she was in her 70s, Tamara Karsavina demonstrated some steps of *batterie* at the barre to Antoinette Sibley, saying, "To get the full benefit from *battements frappés*, we must train our muscles to give a quick reaction. That means that the *dégagé* must be sharp and in the nature of a 'hit out.'" The marveling Ms. Sibley embraced Ms. Karsavina and said, "Oh, Madame, I can never do it like that!"[81]

• Ballet teachers often have a sense of authority. While teaching the Sadler's Wells Royal Ballet, Soulamif Messerer, who had defected from Russia, stressed the importance of the dancers believing they are the characters they are portraying on stage. She once scolded a class, "You don't believe yourself — you must believe yourself. I danced for 25 years as prima ballerina at the Bolshoi. I know everything."[82]

• During the 1940s, Helen Keller, who was both blind and deaf, visited the studio of modern dance choreographer Martha Graham. Eventually, she asked, "What is jumping?" Ms. Graham asked dancer Merce Cunningham to come over, then she placed Ms. Keller's hands on his waist, and Mr. Cunningham jumped in first position. Ms. Keller responded, "How like thought! How like the mind it is!"[83]

• Choreographer Jerome Robbins could be very rude to people, and when he worked for the New York City Ballet, other people sometimes complained to George Balanchine. For example, John Clifford once told Mr. Balanchine, "Mr. B, I don't know what to do about Jerry." Mr. Balanchine replied, "You know, dear, he will teach you how not to treat people."[84]

• Some dance students are very loyal to their teachers. José Limón once overheard a couple of students at the Bennington College of Dance talking together after witnessing a performance of a dance choreographed by Doris Humphrey. One woman said to the other, "I don't know how she can compose so well. She never took lessons from my teacher."[85]

• After discovering the world of dancing in his reading, Kenneth MacMillan decided that he wanted to study dance at the Royal Ballet School. Therefore, he forged a letter from his father and sent it to Ninette de Valois. The forgery succeeded, and he began to study dance. In 1946, he became a founder-member of Sadler's Wells Theatre Ballet. [86]

• A man — who didn't dance — visited the dance class of Margaret Craske. At the end of her class, he said goodbye and jokingly executed a *port de bras*. Quickly, Ms. Craske reached out and corrected the position of the visitor's hand. As you would expect, in her dance classes, she tells her students over and over, "Get it right!"[87]

• Among the many soon-to-be-famous people who studied with modern dance pioneer Martha Graham — and among the earliest — was then-unknown-but-soon-to-be-a-movie-star Bette Davis. Ms. Graham helped Ms. Davis get her first job in acting by teaching her how to fall down several stairs without killing herself.[88]

• William de Mille, the father of Agnes, did not want her to study dance. However, Agnes' younger sister, Margaret, developed fallen arches, and her orthopedist recommended that she study dance. William did not want to treat one daughter differently from the other, so he let Agnes also take dance lessons.[89]

• Ballet teacher Nicolas Legat insisted that dancers learn to move correctly. When established dancer Anna Roje came to him for lessons, he would not allow her to dance but instead insisted that she do only barre work for six months. After her faults had been corrected, she began to dance in his class.[90]

• The great black dancer Bill Robinson, aka Mr. Bojangles, taught dance steps to many people. His usual method was to show them a few dance steps they could do, then show them a few dance steps it was impossible for them to do. He liked for his students to know who the master was.[91]

• Ruth St. Denis once taught Martha Graham an important lesson when Ms. Graham was just starting to dance. Ms. St. Denis told Ms. Graham, "Show me your dance." Ms. Graham replied, "I don't have one," and Ms. St. Denis advised, "Well, dear, go out and *get* one."[92]

Fans

• Mary Lou Raines was a celebrity as a teenager because she was a dancer on *The Buddy Deane Show*, a very popular teenage dance party show in Baltimore, Maryland, from 1957 to 1964. When she first started going with her future husband, he did not know about her celebrity, so he was surprised when everywhere they went, people would say, "There's Mary Lou! There's Mary Lou!" He says, "I wondered if she had just been released from the penitentiary."[93]

• Whenever ballerina Margot Fonteyn danced in Kenneth MacMillan's *Romeo and Juliet*, many of her fans used to skip Act II because "Margot only gets married in it." Instead, they watched Acts I and III because she had much more of a chance to dance and act.[94]

Chapter 3: From Food to Mishaps

Food

• While in Japan, ballerina Nora Kaye faced a problem. She didn't like Japanese food, and she had to attend a party hosted by a Japanese man who was prominent in the dance world. Fortunately, dance impresario Paul Szilard came up with a solution. They pretended that Ms. Kaye was on a strict diet, and whenever she did not want to eat something, she would turn to Mr. Szilard and ask for permission to eat it, but he would reply, "Absolutely not." This worked well for a while, but then Ms. Kaye put on too much of an act, saying that something looked delicious and she wanted to eat it. Mr. Szilard rebelled when she said, "Oh, isn't he awful. He won't let me eat a thing, and I'm starving." Mr. Szilard whispered to her, "Nora, one more crack like that, and I am going to give you permission to eat the fungi." Ms. Kaye then put her hand on his knee and told the host, "He really does take good care of me."[95]

• Monica Lera, a former member of the Opera House Ballet, remembers a time when she and other dancers played children in Act II in *La Bohème* and were required to carry food onto the stage. Because the food was real, tasty, and free, and because the dancers were living on low wages, they nibbled on the food before bringing it in, reasoning that no one in the audience could see that a bite or two had been taken out of a slice of ham or a cream cake. Of course, the singers on stage did notice, and in a low voice would joke to the dancers: "The rats have been at this. I shall complain to the management."[96]

• Mrs. Haskell, the mother of ballet critic Arnold Haskell, enjoyed watching ballet practice at the London dance studio of Princess Seraphine Astafieva. She often rewarded dancers with boxes of chocolates. Because young dance student Patrick Healey-Kay, who later became world famous as Anton Dolin, knew that Mrs. Haskell enjoyed watching the circle of *pirouettes* with which Ms. Astafieva's students ended the class, he sometimes asked Mrs. Haskell what she would give him if he danced two circles of *pirouettes* instead of just one. In that way, he was able to earn many boxes of chocolates.[97]

• While on tour, Merce Cunningham and his dance troupe stopped at the Brownsville Eat-All-You-Want Restaurant, where they wolfed down food in huge quantities. (Dancer Steve Paxton ate five pieces of pie for dessert!) Mr. Cunningham asked the cashier how the restaurant managed to stay open, and she replied, "Most people don't eat as much as you people." On another tour, they stopped at a restaurant that advertised homemade pies. Before the dance troupe left the restaurant, they heard the servers tell the regular pie-eating customers, "I'm sorry — we don't have any more."[98]

• Mikhail Mordkin was jealous of the great success enjoyed by his dance partner, Anna Pavlova, who even had food named after her. While the two were preparing to order supper at a restaurant, Mr. Mordkin glanced at the menu, then he grew angry. He showed the menu to Ms. Pavlova and said, "There you are! Now you see! Frog's legs à la Pavlova! Always it is yourself! Never of Mordkin you think, but always Pavlova, Pavlova, Pavlova! Frog's legs à la Pavlova! But where is there frog's legs à la Mordkin? Where is there anything eatable à la Mordkin? Tell me that!"[99]

• As a young child growing up in Ufa, the great dancer Rudolf Nureyev was frequently hungry. When he started kindergarten, he was always late to class each morning, and his teacher asked him why. Young Rudi explained that he had to eat at home. His teacher then reminded him that he could eat at school. What young Rudi didn't explain was that now he had a chance to eat twice in the morning, he was not going to miss it — especially since he could not be sure that food would be available at home in the evening. (One day in class, he fainted from hunger.)[100]

• Alexandra Danilova lived in Russia after the revolution, so she suffered from food shortages for many years. After leaving Russia and going to Germany, where she danced for the Ballet Russe, she feasted on the food there. One day, she was supposed to rehearse with Anton Dolin, but he looked at her and then told her that he was a dancer and not a piano mover. After that — and after being told by the company that she was not allowed to dance until she lost weight — Ms. Danilova slimmed down.[101]

• As you would expect, surrealist Salvador Dali had some very original ideas for ballets choreographed by Léonide Massine. For a scene in which Theseus kills the Minotaur, Mr. Dali wanted to use a real calf's head from which the dancers would cut pieces of meat and eat them. Mr. Dali and Mr. Massine went to several restaurants to see if they could get a calf's head, but the best the waiters could do for them was to offer them a veal sandwich.[102]

• Professional musicians are often asked to dinner, and after they have eaten, asked to play for their food. At one such dinner, pianist Anton Rubinstein was asked to play a *valse* for such guests as wished to dance. Annoyed, he did play a *valse*, but he introduced so many *rubatos* into it that he made dancing almost impossible. In addition, he started the *valse* at a conventional tempo, but then he speeded it up so much that no one was able to dance to it.[103]

• Like other young energetic dancers, 15-year-old Jacques d'Amboise had to learn to fight dehydration. Quickly, he discovered a system that worked for him, and whenever the servers at a West 56th Street coffee shop near City Center in New York saw him coming, they would set out a glass of grapefruit juice, a glass of milk, and a glass of water — all of which he quickly drank.[104]

• When Josephine Baker was growing up as an impoverished black child in East St. Louis, she and her brothers and sisters used to look through garbage cans, hoping to find something that could be used to make soup — for example, they were very happy when they found some chicken heads. In the 1920s, Ms. Baker conquered Paris as a dancer. [105]

Fouettés

• It's possible for an audience to get distracted by the quantity of dance moves and ignore the dancing itself. For example, in *Swan Lake* the audience tends to count the 32 *fouettés* made by Odile. That's why choreographer George Balanchine allowed very few multiple *pirouettes* in his ballets: "Two, maybe three … after that the audience starts to count." Someone once said to ballerina Alexandra Danilova, "You do such virtuoso dancing, you do impressive *fouetté* turns, but you don't do extreme, multiple *pirouettes* — why?" Ms. Danilova replied, "Because I am too busy dancing."[106]

• Early in her career, Natalia Makarova had great trouble with the 32 *fouettés* in *Swan Lake*. Of course, they are supposed to be performed in one spot, and the ballet dancer ought not to travel around the stage while spinning, but Ms. Makarova remembers that during her first attempt at them on stage she traveled so far that she ended up in a rear wing where she could not be seen by the audience.[107]

• Anna Pavlova didn't like to perform *fouettés*, but that doesn't mean that she couldn't perform them when she wanted. One day, she saw a dancer practicing *fouettés* — but not well. Ms. Pavlova said, "You want to learn *fouetté*? I show you." She performed 64 *fouettés*, then left. [108]

Gays and Lesbians

• As a gay teenager, author Joel Perry used to hide copies of *Playgirl*, which features a nude male centerfold each issue, under his bed. One day, his mother found them, so he told her that he was keeping them for a girl named Susie so that Susie's mother wouldn't find them. His mother believed him. Years later, after he had been living with a male lover for 11 years, she asked him if he was gay. After hearing that he was, she said, "Oh, honey, and you're not even a good dancer." [109]

• Before Stonewall, Edythe Eyde used to go to a gay bar that was divided into two halves. One side was reserved for lesbians, and in the other side sat straight men. One day, a straight man came over and asked several women to dance with him. Being lesbians, they weren't interested. When he reached Ms. Eyde, he said, "What's the matter, lady? Don't you dance with men?" She replied, "Of course not! What kind of a girl do you think I am!"[110]

• The first known lesbian couple to dance at the White House was Barbara Love and Kay Whitlock. Having gone to the White House in 1978 to present President Jimmy Carter with the International Women's Year National Plan of Action, they waltzed together to chamber music in an outer chamber.[111]

Gifts

• Learning to dance ballet with a partner can be difficult. When Chan Hon Goh, later a prima ballerina with the National Ballet of Canada, was learning to dance with Che Chun, she was terrified at first when he lifted her because she was afraid that he would drop her. Eventually, she learned to trust him, and she treasured a swan-shaped mirror he gave her before their first show together. The card that came with the gift said, "May this be a grand *jeté* to a brilliant career." (It was a grand *jeté* to a brilliant career — and more. Later, they married.)[112]

• Early in his career, ballet master George Balanchine made enough money in Copenhagen to buy an American car, which he took to London, then drove onto a ferry and crossed the English channel to France. Unfortunately, once in France, he discovered that he didn't have enough money to pay the import fee, so he handed the car keys to a stranger and then continued on his way, using public transportation. [113]

• Alicia Alonso was born in Cuba, but her grandfather was from Spain. When she was seven years old, Alicia and her family visited Spain. Her grandfather asked them for a present — to bring him back a piece of Spain. Therefore, Alicia and her sister learned some Spanish folk dances that they performed for him when they returned to Cuba. [114]

• When she was a young girl, Moira Shearer once darned a pair of ballet shoes while riding in a bus to her ballet lesson. An old man sat next to her and told her of his interest in ballet. He then stood up, handed her a silver thimble, said, "Keep this for luck, my dear," and disappeared.[115]

Good Deeds

• Modern dance pioneer May O'Donnell and her husband, composer Ray Green, acquired five old, dilapidated townhouses in Manhattan's Lower East Side. Mr. Green devoted time and effort to restoring the townhouses, which Ms. O'Donnell described as looking "as if they were in a Charles Addams cartoon. They were dirty, cobwebbed, dingy, and dank." After restoring the houses, they lived in one, sold two, and gave two away. Ms. O'Donnell explains why they gave two houses away: "... it involved ... helping others find a home. We both had an idea of sharing beyond our own lives. The neighborhood was dreadful, full of drug dealers and dangerous people, but somehow we who lived on this street got together and made it a decent place to live."[116]

• Many dancers show consideration in helping other dancers. When Maria Tallchief gave her first performance in 1951 as Queen of the Swans in George Balanchine's production of *Swan Lake*, things did not go well, and she was dissatisfied with her performance. At 1 a.m., she received a comforting telephone call from retired ballerina Felia Doubrovska, who told her, "I just want you to know, Maria, maybe you're not too happy tonight. But it was nerves."[117]

Husbands and Wives

• When the young ballerina Maria Tallchief was married to choreographer George Balanchine, they hosted a dinner for composer Igor Stravinsky. Mr. Balanchine liked to cook, but he couldn't physically be at home to prepare the food, so he left instructions for Ms. Tallchief, telling her when to start cooking the potatoes, etc. Unfortunately, Ms. Tallchief was so nervous that she dropped the potatoes on the floor, where they rolled everywhere, and when Mr. Stravinsky arrived, she was picking up the potatoes, washing them off, and putting them in a pot. A very embarrassed Ms. Tallchief explained what had happened, and a very polite Mr. Stravinsky said, "The potatoes will taste better."[118]

• People tend to think that celebrities live glamorous lives, but that's not always true — at least not every moment of their lives. When George Balanchine, one of America's greatest choreographers, was married to Maria Tallchief, one of America's greatest ballerinas, the apartment they lived in was on the fifth floor, and they had to walk up five flights of stairs to get to it. In addition, they had to do their own housework. Mr. Balanchine disliked having to walk on newspapers after Ms. Tallchief had scrubbed the floor.[119]

• Dance director Busby Berkeley once liked a woman so much that he walked 10 miles every night to woo her. After doing this for 67 consecutive nights, he gave it up — she had married someone else.[120]

Illnesses and Injuries

• Apparent setbacks may not be true setbacks. In the United States, Mary Anthony once danced some difficult steps well at a rehearsal for the musical *Touch and Go*, which was choreographed by Helen Tamiris. Ms. Anthony kept dancing the difficult steps and suddenly she heard a crack like a board being broken, but it was her foot that was broken — in two places. She could not dance in *Touch and Go*, but the musical's director, George Abbott, witnessed her injury and was so impressed by her dedication that he asked her to stage the musical in London.[121]

• Accidents occur while dancing on stage. At a charity performance, Nicolas Legat was dancing with Olga Preobrazhenskaya when she raised an arm while doing a series of *pirouettes* and accidentally hit him in the mouth, knocking out several of his teeth. Mr. Legat remained calm, kept his mouth tightly closed, and finished the dance. Because of the applause, Ms. Preobrazhenskaya wanted to dance an encore, but she fainted when Mr. Legat spat four teeth out on the floor backstage.[122]

• Nora Kaye was a New York ballerina who mixed classicism on stage with earthiness off stage. Sometimes the two characteristics would meet. A dancer in *Pillar of Fire* once suffered from muscle cramps and had to stumble off stage. Three dancers gathered around to help her — although they were supposed to be dancing with Ms. Kaye on stage. This forced Ms. Kaye to improvise a dance. As she leapt past the just-off-stage group, she asked in an aside, "Where the hell is everybody?"[123]

• Young dancer Alicia Alonso had two operations on her eyes to repair detached retinas, forcing her to lie still for months until the physicians allowed her to get up from bed. As she lay in bed, she practiced dancing using only her fingers, moving them as she visualized the movements of the dancers in such ballets as *Giselle*. When she finally got out of bed, she was unable to stand by herself, but she got herself in shape again and became a world-famous ballerina.[124]

• Agnes de Mille attended the ceremony in which President Gerald Ford presented her fellow choreographer Martha Graham with the Medal of Freedom. (Trivia: President Ford's wife, Betty, had been a dancer for Ms. Graham.) Shortly after the ceremony, Ms. de Mille suffered a major heart attack and went to the hospital, where she complained, "That's what comes from having dinner with a Republican!"[125]

• Anna Pavlova frequently danced when she was injured. After she had injured her left ankle while rehearsing in St. Louis, Missouri, newspaper reporters asked her which ankle she had injured. Ms. Pavlova told them, "The right one." After the reporters had left, she explained to her dancers why she had lied: "Now they will watch the right ankle during the performance, and nothing will seem amiss."[126]

• Watching is an important part of a dancer's education. Ballerina Marion Tait once had a nerve removed from her foot. As soon after the operation as she was able, she hobbled into ballet rehearsal, leaning on a cane and wearing a blue plastic bag on her foot. She then began to watch the rehearsal and so learn the choreography.[127]

• After Margot Fonteyn had retired and was ill, Rudolf Nureyev was speaking with her on the telephone. Worried that her illness might tire her too much, he said, "I should go, or I tire you out." Ms. Fonteyn replied firmly, "Listen. You *never* tire me out. *Never.*"[128]

Language

• When Pierre Monteux was conducting for Sergei Diaghilev, a champion of new choreography and new music, he sometimes ran into problems with orchestras that resented playing some of the new music. For example, at the Vienna Opera House, the Philharmonic Orchestra rebelled at playing Igor Stravinsky's music for *Petrushka*, and so at rehearsals — despite Mr. Monteux's best efforts — the violins, celli, basses, and violas played *pianissimo*, while the woodwinds and brasses played *fortissimo*. Mr. Diaghilev heard the cacophony, and he yelled at Mr. Monteux, "It's not *Petrushka* — it's a funeral march!" The musicians of the Vienna Philharmonic Orchestra, eager for a fight, jumped to their feet and demanded an apology. Mr. Diaghilev agreed to give them an apology, but he knew that they could not understand French when it was spoken quickly, so he proceeded to insult them in the worst and most derogatory terms possible, but he was such a good actor that the musicians thought he was making an apology. The Vienna Philharmonic Orchestra accepted the "apology," the rehearsal went on, but unfortunately, Mr. Monteux says, "The results were dull, uninspired performances because ... the great Vienna Philharmonic simply could not play *Petrushka*."[129]

• Nicolas Legat was a Russian dancer who lived the last years of his life teaching ballet in England. Unfortunately, he didn't learn English very well. One day, he spoke to a police officer, using the words that he had learned so he could greet visitors to his dance studio, "Thank you very much, too much, sit down, please." His lack of English led to some funny sentences. Whenever he wanted to tell a pupil in class to hold her head up, he said, "Keep your football up."[130]

• Gerald Arpino met Princess Margaret on Oct. 27, 1977, at the Contemporary Dance Foundation Gala at the Hotel Pierre. He had always been told that British royalty are impeccable in their pronunciation, and so he practiced perfectly saying, "I — am — pleased — to — meet — you — Your — Royal — Highness." The meeting went very well. Mr. Arpino was impeccable in his pronunciation, and Princess Margaret responded, "How d'ja' do?"[131]

• Alexandra Danilova, from Russia, and Alicia Markova, from England, used to travel throughout the United States and give ballet performances. In the south, waiters often had a hard time understanding Ms. Markova's British accent, so Ms. Danilova would tell the waiter both of their orders, then say about Ms. Markova, "These French girls — they just can't learn to speak good English."[132]

• Andrei Kramarevsky taught classes at the School of American Ballet despite knowing very little English. According to ballerina Darci Kistler, one of his students, he knew only two English words. Dance students who made mistakes, he called "cheap." Dance students who didn't make mistakes, he called "expensive."[133]

• When ballerina Marie Taglioni became pregnant after her marriage, she tried to keep her pregnancy secret by telling other dancers that she had a sore knee. The lie didn't work. The dancers even began to use the term *"mal au genou"* ("hurt knee") as a synonym for being pregnant.[134]

• Alexandre Volinine, the dance partner of Anna Pavlova, did not learn much English. At a restaurant, he would ask for a menu, look intently at it, then point at a random spot on the menu and order, "Ham and eggs."[135]

Media

• The author of this book once wrote a preview story for an Ohio University School of Dance performance. The only place for interviews during a rehearsal was in a closet, so Ohio University dance teacher Michele Geller told the dance students, "This is David Bruce. He is going to interview you for a story he is writing for *The Athens News*, so don't be shocked if he asks you to go into a closet with him."[136]

• A *Sports Illustrated* writer once met ballet dancer Edward Villella for an interview. Immediately after shaking hands, Mr. Villella said, "I know the question you're dying to ask even before you ask it: Am I straight?" (The answer is yes; Mr. Villella is married with children.) [137]

• Loïe Fuller, a 19th- and 20th-century American dancer who took Paris by storm, understood the value of publicity. Whenever public interest in her seemed to be decreasing, she would start a lawsuit or announce that she was suffering from a severe illness.[138]

Mishaps

• Many performing artists desire quiet and privacy before facing an audience. Impresario Sol Hurok once was backstage before a performance by Sadler's Wells Ballet. He knocked on ballerina Margot Fonteyn's door. No answer. He went away, returned a short while later, and knocked again. No answer. He then opened the door and asked if she had heard his knock. Ms. Fonteyn told him, "GET OUT!" After the performance, the two met, and Mr. Hurok asked if she were angry at him. Ms. Fonteyn smiled, then asked, "Why on earth should I be angry at you?" After Mr. Hurok reminded her that she had told him to get out of her dressing room, she replied, "Don't you know that, before a performance, I won't talk to anyone?" After giving him a kiss, she added, "Remember, I don't want to see *anyone* before I go on."[139]

• Soprano Joan Hammond once appeared on the BBC series *Gala Performance* on the same program as ballet dancers Margot Fonteyn and Rudolf Nureyev. Unfortunately, as she was singing, she caught sight of the dancers warming up their muscles at the barre. Normally, this would be OK, but they were warming up using a rhythm that was different from that of the aria that Ms. Hammond was singing, so she had to stop, explain what had happened, apologize, then begin singing again. The aria went well this time, but after the program, the conductor, Malcolm Arnold, told her, "You were lucky, Joan. After Margot and Nureyev moved away from you, they came into *my* vision, and I had to force myself to keep to Puccini and not follow their timing for the entire aria. I didn't want to stop and cause you to start yet again." [140]

• As a young dance student, Peter Martins thought he was both a strong and a good dance partner, but he learned the truth in a performance of August Bournonville's *Far From Denmark*. At one point, the 20 males onstage were required to lift their partners and hold them in the air during the applause that followed. Of all the 20 males, young Peter was the first to lower his partner. She was furious at his weakness and hissed at him, "You need to do push-ups." He cried after the performance, and the next day he bought a piece of exercise equipment known as a chest expander and started to use it and to do push-ups.[141]

• Peter Martins took over as a co-director of the New York City Ballet after George Balanchine's death. For a while, Mr. Martins continued his dancing career, but he soon discovered that it was too difficult to do both jobs. During a performance with Suzanne Farrell, with whom he had had little rehearsal, he had numerous entrances and exits. While he was standing in the wings, he watched an improvising Ms. Farrell and told the ballet mistress, "Doesn't Suzanne look great out there!" The ballet mistress replied, "Yes, but you're supposed to be there with her." Mr. Martins quickly made a belated appearance on stage.[142]

• Disasters and near-disasters are always a possibility at a public dance performance. Ballerina Darci Kistler once was dancing when her costume started to unravel at a side seam. She remembers thinking that even if her costume came off, she had to continue to dance. (Fortunately, this turned out to be a near-disaster rather than a disaster.) On another occasion, the glue on her false eyelashes glued her eyes shut so that she was unable to see on stage. And once when she was a young ballerina, her perspiration caused her mascara to run down her face; after that experience, she used waterproof mascara.[143]

• Before a matinee performance, a young Margot Fonteyn noticed that some other people were taking a drink, so she had a few drinks, too. Big mistake. The other people weren't dancing at the matinee, but she was. Feeling tipsy and inclined to giggle, she went on stage and discovered that her body could not do what she wanted it to do. The performance was a nightmare, and the applause following it was scanty. For the next 30 years of her career, she refused to take even an aspirin before a performance, and she never again drank before a performance. [144]

• Early in her career, dancer Ann Miller performed live on vaudeville bills featuring the Three Stooges. One day, the stage manager forgot to put down a rubber mat that protected the stage when the Three Stooges engaged in a pie-throwing sketch. When Ms. Miller came on the stage to dance, she slipped and fell into the orchestra pit. The Three Stooges thought this was funny, but Ms. Miller was upset and left the stage briefly before returning to dance. Afterward, the Three Stooges sent her flowers and congratulated her for acting so professionally by performing after the mishap.[145]

• While filming *Follow the Fleet* in 1936, Fred Astaire suffered a mishap while dancing with Ginger Rogers. She was wearing a beaded gown, and the right sleeve hit Mr. Astaire's head, dazing him. However, he continued dancing. Although they made 30 takes of the dance, the best take was the one in which Mr. Astaire carried on despite being dazed.[146]

• Ivan Nagy once danced with Margot Fonteyn in Puerto Rico. They were scheduled to dance at a university, but because of a strike they were forced to dance on an emergency stage at a Holiday Inn with low ceilings. At one point, Mr. Nagy was supposed to pick up

Ms. Fonteyn and run with her. He began running, but suddenly she was no longer in his hands. Looking back, he saw her hanging from a chandelier.[147]

• Ballet dancer Rudolf Nureyev could be cocky. In 1963, after a late performance, he was walking in Toronto, Canada, when he began to dance up the centerline of a street. A police officer arrested him, and Mr. Nureyev said, "You can't arrest me. I'm Rudolf Nureyev." The police officer replied, "Yeah, and I'm Fred Astaire — but *you* are under arrest." Mr. Nureyev was taken away in handcuffs.[148]

• For a while, Oscar-winning actress Goldie Hawn was a chorus girl. While dancing in the chorus of the musical *Kiss Me, Kate*, she witnessed an actor who played a strongman run into a problem. He couldn't find his costume — a loincloth — so he ended up appearing on stage while wearing a woman's leotard. Ms. Hawn says, "I laughed so hard I peed down my leg."[149]

• Nora Kaye was a very energetic ballerina. Once, while dancing in Valerie Bettis' *Streetcar Named Desire*, she accidentally knocked out her partner, Igor Youskevitch, forcing her to finish the rape scene by herself. [150]

• Edward Renton once conducted a dance with such a slow tempo that dancer Robert Helpmann, who tried mightily to jump to the music, complained, "Have you never heard of gravity?"[151]

Chapter 4: From Money to Programs

Money

• A society woman once made the mistake of announcing that Anna Pavlova would dance at one of her affairs. Afterward, she asked Ms. Pavlova how much she would charge for a dance, and she was shocked when Ms. Pavlova said the price would be £500. The society woman asked, "Surely £500 is a very great deal of money for a performance which will last only five or six minutes?" Ms. Pavlova stood firm, and since the society woman had already announced that Ms. Pavlova would dance, she was forced to agree to Ms. Pavlova's price. However, Ms. Pavlova thought for a moment about the kind of guests who would likely be present at the society woman's party, then she said, "If you do not insist upon my sitting with your friends at supper, I will reduce my fee to £300."[152]

• Léonide Massine choreographed "The Dying Swan" for Anna Pavlova, and the only two people he taught it to were Ms. Pavlova and his wife. However, when his student Patricia Bowman expressed an interest in learning to dance "The Dying Swan," he asked his wife for permission to teach it to her. She agreed — provided that Ms. Bowman paid $300 for the privilege. After Ms. Bowman had paid the fee and had learned the dance, Mr. Massine said she might forget some of the steps, so he handed her a book that had photographs of "The Dying Swan" and descriptions of all its steps — Ms. Bowman could have learned the dance merely from reading the book! In addition, Mr. Massine charged her $5 for the book![153]

• Dancer Ida Rubinstein was immensely wealthy. Her estate had greenhouses growing flowers of many different colors, and her flower gardens were designed so that the flowers could be replaced so that their color would match the color of her dress when she was entertaining. In addition, she filled a room with rows and rows of boxes set on shelves. Each box contained a hat, a pair of gloves, and a pair of shoes in matching colors.[154]

• American dance pioneer Ted Shawn traveled the world looking for inspiration for new dances. While in Rangoon, he watched some Burmese dancers. A man in the audience threw some money on the stage, and a dancer picked the money up. The man in the audience yelled, "What do I get for that?" The dancer put the money in her bodice and then replied, "Only a receipt."[155]

• Caroline Otéro, a dancer, once advised Sidonie-Gabrielle Colette, a dancer and writer, "Don't forget, there is always a moment in a man's life, even if he's a miser, when he opens his hands wide ...." Ms. Colette guessed, "In the moment of passion?" Ms. Otéro replied, "No — the moment when you twist his wrist."[156]

• Getting money for dates can be tough. The young composer Giacomo Puccini once pawned his coat to get enough money to take a ballerina out.[157]

• Dancer Ann Pennington felt that the best writer in the world was George White — because he wrote her paychecks.[158]

Mothers

• When dancer Norma Miller was born on December 2, 1919 (before the days of Welfare), her father had recently died, and things were tough. Her mother, an African American, had a hard time trying to work and raise an infant at the same time, so she decided to put her daughter in an orphanage. However, at the orphanage, a little girl pulled on her skirt and asked if she was her Mama. This made her think about her daughter wondering who her mother was, and she said, "I've changed my mind. I'll suck salt before I'll ever leave my children in an orphanage. I'll never separate us ever!" She kept her word, and she kept her family together.[159]

• As a boy, Patrick Healey-Kay — better known as Anton Dolin — studied under Mme. Seraphina Astafieva. Her way of pointing out mistakes was to rap her dancers on the legs. Her very best dancers were the ones who got the most raps because she wanted them to correct their mistakes and improve their dancing. Pat's mother once said, "Pat must have pleased her greatly because his legs were always black and blue!"[160]

Movies

• While touring with the Ballet Russe de Monte Carlo, dancers sometimes whiled away the time before a performance by watching a movie — often the movie was being shown in the same theater they would dance in later that night. One day, the Ballet Russe manager, David Libidins, became irate because the film was still being shown when the stage should have been in the process of being prepared for the ballet that night. Although the movie theater manager told him that an audience was still watching the movie, he strode to the front of the theater and ordered that the lights be turned on. When they were turned on, he was astonished to see that the audience for the movie consisted solely of ballet dancers. For a long time after that, the ballet dancers were forbidden to watch movies.[161]

• Peggygene Evans had a career dancing in the early days of the talkies — and in silent movies. Her manager was her Aunt Ida, who made sure to protect her from Hollywood producers' casting couches. Whenever Aunt Ida negotiated a deal, she always asked, "Now, are there any strings attached?" If strings were attached, no deal was made. Ms. Evans danced in Lon Chaney's *Phantom of the Opera*, and she danced in the first talkie, *The Jazz Singer*. The 4-foot-11 woman had a childlike quality and when she was 44 years old, she was able to double for 10-year-old Shirley Temple in the dance scenes for *The Little Princess*.[162]

• As a ballerina in the former Soviet Union, Natalia Makarova was asked to star in a movie of *Swan Lake*. However, she discovered the movie director lacked taste, although he thought he could teach her how to dance the role of Odile. When he told her, "Dance as if you wanted to seduce me," she replied, "I haven't the slightest desire to do that to you," and then she walked off the set and refused to return. The director was forced to find another ballerina to dance the role of Odile.[163]

• Whenever Fred Astaire was ready to shoot a big dance number for one of his films, word would go out across the studio, and lots of people would come around to watch the dancing. Anthony Perkins was doing a Western while Mr. Astaire was filming *Funny Face* with Audrey Hepburn, and he remembers lots of gunslingers watching the filming of "Clap Yo' Hands."[164]

• The year 1940 was a very bad year for Fred Astaire, who starred in the turkey *Second Chorus*, but it was a very good year for his former dance partner Ginger Rogers. When she won the Best Actress Oscar for her performance in *Kitty Foyle*, Mr. Astaire sent her this one-word telegram: "OUCH."[165]

Names

• The mother of the great tap dancer Savion Glover, one of the creators of *Bring in 'da Noise, Bring in 'da Funk*, knew he was special when she was pregnant with him. In fact, his name comes from a religious vision his mother had — she saw God writing a name on a blackboard: SAVIOR. She read the name, then said, "Now, You know I can't name him Savior." Therefore, she substituted an "n" for the "r." To a great extent, Mr. Glover has been the savior of modern-day tap dancing, bringing it into the era of hip-hop.[166]

• Edward Villella and other dancers called ballerina Melissa Hayden "Old Ironsides" as an affectionate mark of respect for her hard work and determination. One of the things she did to get energy for dancing was to inject herself with vitamin B12. One day, thinking Mr. Villella needed some extra energy, she told him, "Honey, take down your pants." He obeyed her — and was rewarded with a needle in his butt.[167]

• Russian ballet dancer Elena Lukom ran into a problem when she performed in Sweden because audience members laughed when she was introduced. Fortunately, she was able to solve that problem easily. She discovered that in Swedish her last name meant "rest room," so whenever she toured in Sweden, she changed her last name to Lukova. [168]

• Loïe Fuller started a dancing school whose pupils danced for her. The pupils' real names were kept secret from the general public on the grounds that they were from prominent families that might be embarrassed by the publicity, and on the dance programs they were given pseudonyms such as Buttercup, Chocolate, Peach, Pinky, and Smiles.[169]

Native Americans

• When the Native American tribe known as the Wampanoag dance, they dance both clockwise and counterclockwise. When they dance clockwise, they are thanking the good spirits. When they dance counterclockwise, they are paying respect to the other spirits — the evil ones.[170]

• According to many Native Americans of Canada, the Northern Lights are a dance. When the Northern Lights appear in the sky, one sees the spirits of the ancestors dancing.[171]

Nudity

• The costumes for Bronislava Nijinska's *Les Biches* underwent several changes before the ballet's premiere. The costume worn by dancer Vera Nemchinova originally was a full-length evening dress; however, costume designer Marie Laurencin very quickly cut off the train. Ballet producer Sergei Diaghilev then cut off the rest of the skirt. When Ms. Nemchinova complained that the costume made her feel naked, Mr. Diaghilev told her to buy a pair of gloves.[172]

• Sometimes what you think you see is not what you actually see. To create an illusion of nudity, female dancers sometimes wear flesh-colored costumes on which nipples and navels have been painted. Sometimes what you think you see is what you actually see. In 1978, Vivi Flindt stripped off all her clothing to perform the dance of Salome for the Royal Danish Ballet. Her husband, Flemming Flindt, danced the role of Herod.[173]

• When Russian heiress Ida Rubinstein wished to dance nude in the role of Salome in 1908, her brother-in-law, a physician, was so upset that he committed her to a mental institution. It didn't work. After she got out of the mental institution, she appeared nude in many roles, including that of Cleopatra.[174]

• As Rudolf Nureyev was dancing in Tchaikovsky's *Sleeping Beauty* at the Metropolitan Opera, a naked man streaked across the stage. Mr. Nureyev — a homosexual — was delighted.[175]

Old Age

• In his old age, dancer Léonide Massine went to San Francisco to recreate his choreography of *Le Beau Danube*. During his stay at the Valley View Lodge, videotapes of him giving lessons to several dancers were shown, causing some elderly residents to ask, "Did you ever dance, Mr. Massine?" He smiled at the question, replied, "A little," and then he taught the elderly residents a few exercises to lessen their pain from arthritis. Shortly thereafter, the elderly residents came to Mr. Massine and thanked him for his help, saying such things as, "I can move now. Thank you so much for your help — it is better than medicine."[176]

• Modern dance pioneer José Limón once lived temporarily at the Ruxton Hotel on West 77th Street in New York City — a hotel where many retirees lived. As a dancer/choreographer, Mr. Limón was surrounded each day at work by bodies that were nearly perfect, and he was shocked by the bodies of the retirees. Sometimes, he wondered what they had done with their lives to have ended up with such grotesque bodies.[177]

Photographs

• Many dance photographs of Anna Pavlova exist, but people often don't realize how much work went into taking them. The art of photography was in its infancy, and to get an adequate exposure, Ms. Pavlova sometimes had to hold a pose for 20 seconds. To get a photograph of Ms. Pavlova jumping, the photographer was forced to string her up on clotheslines.[178]

• Gordon Anthony's book *A Camera at the Ballet: Pioneer Dancers of the Royal Ballet* did much to give credit to these dance pioneers. Such credit was sorely needed, as a young Royal Ballet School dancer saw a photograph of one of her teachers (a dance pioneer) and exclaimed, "Goodness, were *you* once a dancer!"[179]

Practical Jokes

• Karen Kain once played a practical joke during a dress rehearsal for *Sleeping Beauty*. Of course, she was dancing the role of the princess Aurelia, but she dressed herself in horn-rimmed glasses, the witch Carabosse's fright wig, and bright blue leg warmers for the scene when her dance partner, Frank Augustyn, awakens her with a kiss. The joke amused everyone — except for management, who reprimanded her the following day for not setting a good example for the younger dancers. [180]

• In 1966, while acting in George Bernard Shaw's *You Never Can Tell*, Sir Ralph Richardson fooled the younger members of the cast by telling them anecdotes about dancing with Fred Astaire. They believed him until he went too far and told them he had also danced with Nijinsky.[181]

Prejudice

• Sir Rudolf Bing was the major force behind the integration of the Metropolitan Opera. For example, after being hired as general manager in 1950, he immediately hired the first African-American ballet dancer to dance at the Met — Janet Collins, who danced in the triumphal scene in *Aida*. How did he get around the board of the Metropolitan Opera, which might have opposed the hiring of Ms. Collins? Simple. Sir Rudolf says, "I told the board about it *after* the contract was signed." Sir Rudolf also was responsible for signing the first African American who sang opera at the Met: Marian Anderson, who sang the part of Ulrica in *Un Ballo in Maschera*.[182]

• The great black dancer Bill Robinson, aka Mr. Bojangles, fought prejudice. One day, some members of Duke Ellington's band ordered coffee and doughnuts but were refused service. They ran into Mr. Bojangles and told him what had happened. He told them to follow him, and they all went back to the restaurant. Mr. Bojangles sat down, pulled out his gold-plated gun with the pearl handles, laid the gun on the table, and ordered coffee and doughnuts for himself and his friends. This time, they were served.[183]

• After turning age 13 in 1930, Wah Ming Chang took dancing lessons in a school in California. Unfortunately, soon he was told to leave and never come back. Later, he found out that some parents had complained after discovering that their daughters were dancing with a boy of Asian heritage. As an adult, Mr. Chang became a famous artist and award-winning creator of special effects for such television series as *Star Trek* and such movies as *The Time Machine*.[184]

• In the Jim Crow days, black dance pioneer Katherine Dunham toured the South, where she often confronted race prejudice. In a segregated theater in Louisville, Kentucky, she was outraged because blacks were forced to sit in the balcony. After the performance, she stood on stage, looked at the white members of the audience, and stated, "This is the last time we shall play Louisville because the management refuses to let people like us sit by people like you."[185]

• During the Jim Crow days, Sir Rudolf Bing took the Metropolitan Opera's production of *Aida* on tour to Washington, where he was informed that Janet Collins, the Met's African-American ballerina, would not be welcome at a party at the Mayflower Club. Therefore, Sir Rudolf stayed away from that party and hosted his own, at which Ms. Collins was very welcome.[186]

• In 1937, while traveling in the pre-civil rights south, Norma Miller and some other touring Lindy Hop dancers stopped at a White Castle hamburger joint to order food, only to be told, "We don't serve

Negroes here." One of the dancers replied, "We don't eat Negroes — just serve us a burger!"[187]

Problem-Solving

• Comedian Fanny Brice always had a talent for singing, but she soon realized that her weakness was dancing — a weakness for which George M. Cohan once fired her from the chorus line of one of his shows. Being ambitious, Fanny began to work on her weakness. Before leaving on tour with a show, the young Fanny went through her family's home and gathered up all the female undergarments she could find, using the excuse that as the star of the show she had to make many costume changes and couldn't possibly wear the same bloomers during an entire show. (Actually, she had only one song in the show.) On the road, she began to ask girls in the chorus to teach her dance steps in return for the undergarments. As soon as one girl got tired of teaching her, Fanny would offer some bloomers to another girl. In time, she learned to dance.[188]

• Fern Helsher, an attractive woman, worked as a press agent for Ted Shawn at his dance retreat, a former farm called Jacob's Pillow. One day, a road crew was putting tar topping on the road by Jacob's Pillow, but they were stopping about 100 feet from the driveway leading to Jacob's Pillow. Mr. Shawn mentioned to Ms. Helsher that he had asked the town officials to extend the tar topping another 100 feet, but they were unwilling to do so. Ms. Helsher said, "Let me handle this." She then dressed very provocatively, mixed a pitcher of martinis, and went down to the road crew. She stood at the point to which Mr. Shawn wanted the tar topping poured and told the members of the road crew, "If you build the road to this line, you can have everything you see just beyond it." The road crew raced to build the road, and when they had finished, Ms. Helsher put down the pitcher of martinis and ran to safety.[189]

• Alexandra Danilova once requested her partner, Edouard Borovansky, to not clown around in the background while she danced her variation in *Le Beau Danube*. He replied that he didn't even notice when he was clowning around because he was so carried away by the role. Therefore, the next time Mr. Borovansky clowned around, Ms. Danilova slapped him. Of course, he asked her why she had slapped him, and she replied, "Oh, did I? I was so carried away by my role; I didn't even notice it."[190]

• As a ballerina who danced the part of Odette, the Swan Princess, in *Swan Lake*, Cynthia Gregory was always careful to never get a tan. In the glare of the blue stage lights, a ballerina with a tan under her white makeup would look purple. In addition, after years of performing, Ms. Gregory learned to place her personal items — hair spray, makeup, comb and brush, etc. — in the same place each time on her makeup table so she could quickly find what she wanted, even when she is in a new theater.[191]

• In George Balanchine's *Prodigal Son*, a single stage prop served many uses. It was used to represent a fence with a gate, a banquet table, a rostrum, and a boat, with the Siren's red cloak serving as a sail. The prop served these uses partly out of necessity. The boat that was to be used in the production was not finished in time, so Mr. Balanchine decided to use the stage prop he already had. This worked out so well that the boat was never used, even when it was finished.[192]

• Anna Pavlova's dance troupe spent years touring the United States and appeared in many small towns as well as big cities. Of course, many mishaps arose and many problems had to be solved during those tours. Once, the power went off just as their performance was about to start. Stagehands borrowed several cars and parked them where the headlights would cast light on the stage through the theater's doors and windows. The show went on.[193]

• While touring in South America, the ballet team of Alicia Alonso and Igor Youskevitch was confronted by an abusive audience member in a very crowded stadium. The other audience members solved the problem by grabbing the offensive man, hoisting him high, then passing him above their heads until finally they threw him over a wall and outside the stadium.[194]

• One of the artworks owned by choreographer Léonide Massine was a drawing by Pablo Picasso that showed a satyr raping a nymph. Mr. Massine's cleaning woman in London looked at the drawing and then told him, "Either that goes, or I do." Because he needed a cleaning woman, Mr. Massine packed up the drawing and sent it to his home in Italy.[195]

• Ballerina Yvette Chauviré once averted a disaster on stage. While dancing the lead in *Giselle*, her pearl necklace broke and fell to the floor. Improvising a dance step, Ms. Chauviré swept the necklace to the side of the stage, out of the way of the other dancers, and then continued her performance.[196]

Programs

• Alicia Markova felt strongly about *Giselle* and did much to make it a staple of ballet. During a season of the Markova-Dolin Ballet, the other directors out-voted her and said that *Giselle* would not be performed that season. However, Ms. Markova forced the other directors to change their minds by threatening to jump off her dressing room balcony if *Giselle* were not put in the season's schedule.[197]

• Anna Pavlova was famous for her dance interpretation of Camille Saint-Saëns' "Dying Swan." After Ms. Pavlova's death, choreographer Michel Fokine asked ballerina Alicia Markova to revive "The Dying Swan," but she declined to do so until a note was put in the program saying that the dance was dedicated to the memory of Ms. Pavlova.[198]

• World-renowned choreographer Antony Tudor once attended an all-Tudor program put on by American Ballet Theatre. Afterward, he overheard a member of the audience say, "Three Tudor ballets in one evening! That's a bit much, isn't it?" Mr. Tudor said that after hearing this, he "agreed wholeheartedly."[199]

• Léonide Massine choreographed *La Boutique Fantasque* for — of course — humans. Believe it or not, while Mr. Massine was in residence in San Francisco in 1977, when a version of the dance was performed at the Rossmoor Miniature Theatre, the dancers were puppets![200]

49

Chapter 5: From Rehearsals to Work

Rehearsals

• George Balanchine's New York City Ballet once needed a leading dancer to perform as Apollo at short notice, and Peter Martins, a young dancer with the Royal Danish Ballet, was called in to dance. Everything seemed to Mr. Martins to go well at the first performance, and the critics agreed, but the next day at rehearsal Mr. Balanchine said to him, "Before we begin, you know, you do it all wrong." Then Mr. Balanchine showed him what he wanted. (Mr. Martins says he got the impression during the rehearsal that perhaps the one thing he had done right was to show up for the performance.) Later, Mr. Balanchine told Mr. Martins' teacher, Stanley Williams, that he had been impressed with the young dancer at the rehearsal: "I changed everything, and he remembered everything." This led to Mr. Martins being asked to join the New York City Ballet.[201]

• Anna Pavlova's dance company once arrived in Washington, D.C., for a three-day engagement, but the ballet master neglected to call for a morning rehearsal — an oversight the dancers gleefully took advantage of. Arriving at the theater that evening with only minutes left to put on makeup and costumes, the dancers were confronted by Ms. Pavlova, who told them to form a straight line on the stage, then asked, "Have *you* practiced today?" All of the dancers were forced to admit that they had not. Ms. Pavlova then said, "I am Anna Pavlova — *you* are my *corps de ballet*. I practice every day while *you* do nothing — we will have a lesson here and now." She then made her dancers practice for half an hour, despite the audience members who were impatiently stamping their feet on the other side of the curtain while waiting for the performance to begin.[202]

• Opera singer Mary Garden sometimes watched rehearsals of the Ballets Russes with Sergei Diaghilev, and she noticed just how much attention to detail he paid. On one occasion, he noticed a tiny flower in a dancer's hair and ordered her to remove it because the color wasn't right. Ms. Garden asked him, "Don't you ever rest?" Mr. Diaghilev replied, "My dear Mary, there is all eternity to rest." Ms. Garden writes, "I don't wonder it was the greatest ballet company in the world."[203]

• Buddy Ebsen is perhaps most famous for his role as Jed Clampett on *The Beverly Hillbillies*; however, he and Vilma Ebsen were a famous brother-and-sister dance team during the 1930s. Frequently, they rehearsed in hot, unventilated rehearsal halls, leaving pools of sweat on the floor. Other people used to come into the rehearsal hall, look at the pools of sweat on the floor, and ask, "Were the Ebsens here?"[204]

• At a ballet rehearsal in London, Sergei Diaghilev suddenly asked Leon Bakst, "What are the three most beautiful things in this theatre today?" Then he answered his own question, "[Ballerina] Olga Spessiva, the little boy with the big brown eyes, and me." The "little boy with the big brown eyes" was Anton Dolin, who became famous throughout the world as a ballet dancer.[205]

• When it came to his dancing, Fred Astaire was a perfectionist. He sometimes rehearsed 18 hours a day, losing up to 15 pounds in the process. In addition, when his dancing partners rehearsed with him, at the end of the practice, they would sometimes find blood in their shoes. Mr. Astaire once explained why he rehearsed so much: "I wanted to make it good, then make it better."[206]

• Ballerina Natalia Makarova was rehearsing *Manon* when the orchestra suddenly began playing an unexpected piece of music. She felt bad because this meant she wasn't sufficiently familiar with the music of the ballet, but then she saw everyone smiling at her and realized that the orchestra was playing "Happy Birthday."[207]

• Anna Pavlova took dance rehearsals seriously. Early in her career, she arrived at the Mariinsky Theatre, but she discovered that she had forgotten her practice clothes. No problem. She wrapped two towels around her body and practiced — despite the sniggering of the stagehands in the theater.[208]

Religion

• After Rumi, the founder of the Whirling Dervishes, died, zealots went to the ruler and asked him to suppress Rumi's innovations of sacred dance and sacred music. The ruler, being a wise man, asked a learned man, the Mufti of Qonya, Sheik Sadru-'d-Din, if he should listen to the zealots. The Mufti told him, "Do nothing of the kind. Listen not to such biased suggestions. There is an apostolical saying to this effect: 'A laudable innovation, introduced by a perfect follower of the prophets, is of the same nature with the customary practices of the prophets themselves.'" The ruler took the Mufti's advice and did not suppress the Whirling Dervishes' sacred dance and sacred music.[209]

• Dance is sometimes liturgical. At a Catholic Church, a young female dancer rhythmically moved down the aisle, then laid a lily at the bishop's feet. The bishop joked to the pastor, "If she asks for your head on a platter, she can have it."[210]

Respect

• Even at very young ages, ballet dancers can command attention. While Antoinette Sibley was still at the British junior ballet school — the White Lodge — the ballet students were excited over a program listing all the dancers, even the minor ones, of a performance of *The Sleeping Beauty*. The excitement was not over the dancers performing Aurora or the Prince but over a dancer with a minor role — "Antoinette Sibley is a Lilac Fairy attendant!"[211]

• Soviets respect ballet. To correctly film a scene in *Romeo and Juliet*, ballerina Galina Ulanova had to run 70 or 80 yards several times. At first, a group of watching sailors applauded each time she made the run, then they began to worry that she might exhaust herself. One sailor told choreographer Leonid Lavrovsky, "If you kill her, we'll kill you."[212]

• When Eleanora Hughes was dancing in Paris, a Spanish marquis fell in love with her and threatened to jump out of a window unless she returned his love. She told him, "All right, dear, go ahead and jump. But since the room is only two stories above the ground, I'm not the least impressed by your bravery."[213]

Retirement

• This anecdote is touching rather than funny. Modern dance pioneer Martha Graham danced until she was 75, and she took her retirement from dance hard, although she continued to teach and to choreograph. One day, Tim Wengerd, a dancer in her company, saw that she had been crying, and she explained that she had been dreaming that she was dancing — something she was now incapable of doing in real life.[214]

• As the great dancer Rudolf Nureyev edged closer to his 50th birthday, critics began to say that it was time for him to retire. However, Mr. Nureyev declined to stop dancing. Instead, he said, "Inside, I am only twenty-three, an eternal youth. Dancing, for me, is forever."[215]

Sabotage

• During her performance in the ballet *Firebird* in New York, Irina Baronova leaped onto the stage, only to have her shoulder straps break and the top of her costume fall down. Her dance partner, Paul Petroff, reached under her arm and held up her costume while she finished the dance. Later, they examined her costume and discovered that it had been sabotaged — a razor blade had been used to almost sever the shoulder straps.[216]

• After ballerina Marie Taglioni made her triumphant debut at the Paris Opéra, several ballet dancers became so jealous that before her next performance, they sprinkled bits of soap on the stage in the hope that she would slip on them.[217]

Sex

• Dance impresario Paul Szilard once saw ballerina Nora Kaye wearing lots of jewels, and he asked her, "Nora, are these faux, or are they real?" She replied, "Darling, they're real." The fabulous jewelry had come from rich man Harry Winston, who unfortunately did not pay for it, and who later asked for it back. Ms. Kaye did not want to return the jewelry. This led to a lawsuit, and the judge ruled against Ms. Kaye, forcing her to return the jewelry. When Mr. Szilard asked what had happened, Ms. Kaye replied simply, "Well, my dear, I f**ked for nothing."[218]

• Martha Graham once lectured at a Texas university where Tommy Tune was studying. She told the dance students in a lecture, "All great dance stems from the lonely place." One of the dance students said, "Miss Graham, you said that all great dancing stems from the lonely place. Where is the lonely place?" Ms. Graham replied, "Between your legs. Next question." According to Mr. Tune, "We were never the same again."[219]

• American dance pioneer Ted Shawn once choreographed the bawdy ancient Greek comedy *Lysistrata*, in which the Spartan and Athenian women decide to stop the Peloponnesian War by declining to have sex until the war ends. According to Mr. Shawn, the young dancers of his company claimed to have "learned about life from the birds, the bees, the flowers, and the *Lysistrata* ballet."[220]

• While watching David Lichine dance in *L'Apres-Midi d'un Faune*, photographer/writer Gordon Anthony never wondered why the nymph ran after dropping her scarf![221]

• Ford Madox Ford once told a story about an old lady who, after watching a couple dance the tango, said, "I suppose it's all right — if they really love each other."[222]

Swan Lake

• Cynthia Gregory was able to dance the role of Odette/Odile in *Swan Lake* in only her second year with American Ballet Theatre when David Blair of The Royal Ballet staged a new production. She was chosen to be one of the dancers who would understudy the role. Three of the dancers had to stop understudying the role, then a fourth understudy became pregnant. This left the ballerina and two understudies, including Ms. Gregory. However, tickets for *Swan Lake* sold briskly, and ABT decided to add two more performances and let all three dancers undertake the role.[223]

• Rudolf Nureyev and Margot Fonteyn were wonderful partners in ballet, but they differed artistically. Before they first performed *Swan Lake* together, Mr. Nureyev was worried. While dancing in *Swan Lake*, Ms. Fonteyn used much mime, telling the story in gestures, and Mr. Nureyev worried that he "would feel silly standing about" in the mime scenes, and so he told her, "I am afraid I will ruin your *Swan Lake*." Looking him straight in the eyes, Ms. Fonteyn (amiably — but firmly) replied, "Just you try."[224]

Tap Dance

• Peg Leg Bates lost his leg when he was a child working in a cottonseed gin during World War I. However, he didn't let it stop him. His uncle made a peg leg for him — possible because his leg was amputated below the knee — and he learned how to tap dance, using the peg leg to create a heavy, distinctive beat. He was so successful that he appeared on Ed Sullivan's variety television show a total of 21 times — more than any other tap dancer.[225]

• Back in the glory days of tap dancing, dancers would sometimes try to "steal steps" from other dancers. Tap great John Bubbles enjoyed playing a practical joke on other tappers. He would sit in the front row of a vaudeville theater, and when the tap dancer performed Mr. Bubbles took out a pencil and a notebook and pretended to diagram the dancer's steps. Often, the dancer would speed up to stop the "thievery."[226]

• Comedian Lily Tomlin used to do some weird stunts when she was starting out in show business. For example, she used to tap dance while barefoot — after gluing taps to the soles of her feet.[227]

Tempi

• Early in his career, pianist Denis Matthews played the music for a performance by German dancer Annie Fligg. Unfortunately, during the performance, a misunderstanding occurred. In one dance, each time she came by Mr. Matthews, she hissed the word "fast!" at him. Mr. Matthews thought that she was telling him to go fast, so he speeded up the music. Actually, she was trying to tell him that the music was too fast. (Fortunately, she survived the dance, although the tempo almost caused her to have a heart attack.)[228]

• Sir Thomas Beecham once conducted a performance of Mili Balakireff's *Tamara*, but he did not make concessions to the dancers; instead, if anything, he speeded up the tempo, making the dancers work very hard to keep up with the music. After the piece was finished, Sir Thomas said, "That made the buggers hop!"[229]

Theater

• August Wilson has written many plays about the Black Experience, including *The Piano Lesson*, in which Charles S. Dutton danced with his back to the audience. Caricaturist Sam Norkin felt that this was a brilliant idea, as it kept a serious play from appearing to be a musical. However, later Mr. Norkin learned that Mr. Dutton danced in this way because he was "bashful" about his dancing, although the play's director, Lloyd Richards, wanted him to face the audience.[230]

• A Broadway show called *Strike Me Pink* had a chorus line that consisted mostly of the girlfriends of the financial backers of the show. One backer of the show, Waxey Gordon, saw a pretty chorus girl in the show and asked whose girlfriend she was. Informed that she wasn't anyone's girlfriend, he asked, "Then how the hell did she get into the show?"[231]

• Sir Ralph Richardson once toured in William Shakespeare's *Midsummer Night's Dream* in Quito, Ecuador, where the dancing fairies had a rough time because of the high altitude and the lack of oxygen. Quickly, the company learned to put oxygen tanks behind the trees, so the fairies could breathe in extra oxygen before dancing.[232]

Travel

• George Balanchine wanted his dancers to learn from the places they traveled. Once, Patricia Neary was in Rome, teaching a ballet by

Mr. Balanchine. She telephoned him to talk about the dancers, but Mr. Balanchine asked, "Pat, but what about Rome? What have you seen?" She honestly answered, "Nothing." Mr. Balanchine then said, "Forget about my ballet! You're only in Rome once. Go out and look at the beauty of Rome. The sculptures, the fountains, the Sistine Chapel — Rome. Learn!" She did.[233]

• Anna Pavlova took her dance troupe to Japan, where H. Algeranoff purchased a cup with a design of blue reeds against a cream background for only twopence. To the Japanese, the cup was nothing special, but to foreigners, it bore the mark of perfection. Ms. Pavlova admired the cup, then she told Mr. Algeranoff, "You know, Algy, there is nothing in this country that one wants to throw away."[234]

• Being young and ignorant has its advantages. At the very beginning of her career, in 1928, modern dance pioneer May O'Donnell crossed the Atlantic in a ship. A very bad storm — which she called "one of the worst storms in the century" — occurred, and because she and the other young dancers did not realize in how much danger they were, they thought the rolling of the ship in the storm was fun.[235]

• In London, while dancing *Giselle*, Alicia Markova performed on a stage that used lifts — remarkable for their speed — to ascend Giselle from the grave to the world of the spirits known as Wilis. One performance, as she stepped onto the lift, one of the stagehands said, "Here goes the last jet to Wili-Land!"[236]

• When Maria Tallchief joined the Ballet Russe de Monte Carlo as a 17-year-old, she was untraveled. On her first train trip with the troupe, she spent all of the first night sitting straight up in her seat — because she didn't know how to make it recline and she didn't want to ask anyone for help.[237]

• When Antony Tudor first came to the United States, he arrived on Columbus Day. All the banks were closed, and no bonds had been posted, so he was forced to remain on Ellis Island that night. Fortunately, he enjoyed the company he found there.[238]

• As Josephine Baker was leaving a nightclub in Zagreb, Yugoslavia, a student stabbed himself out of love for her. Later, she remarked, "What I like about Europe is the excitement. Something new happens every day."[239]

• When Rudolf Nureyev owned the island of Li Galli, a boat filled with tourists would occasionally sail around the island. Mr. Nureyev often lay in bed, listening as the boat's tour guide recited his accomplishments.[240]

War

• In 1946, when Nora Kaye and Muriel Bentley were dancing in England shortly after World War II, they were only partially prepared for wartime austerity. For example, realizing that the food options might be limited at the Savoy where they were staying, they asked the waiter what they could have for breakfast. The waiter replied that they could have anything they wanted, so they ordered eggs. However, as the waiter was leaving, he asked, "May I have the eggs now, please?" Another problem they ran into was wearing a wardrobe that was sumptuous in England at that time. They wore high heels, nylons, silk dresses, and fur jackets, and they were frequently propositioned because other people assumed that anyone with such fine clothing in a society with clothing rationing had to belong to a profession that welcomes propositions.[241]

• During World War II, ballet dancer Valentina Pereyaslavec suffered enormous privations, including being incarcerated in a camp for Ukrainian displaced persons. When she finally made her way to the United States, she had $11, a coffee pot, a winter coat (made from a blanket originally belonging to the German army), and two left shoes — the only shoes that were available to her.[242]

• War is hell, including hell on male ballet dancers. For one thing, male dancers, like other males, often must go off to fight the war. For another, food is often scarce during war. When British dance critic Arnold L. Haskell saw some American dancers during World War II, he noticed immediately that they were well nourished, in contrast to the British male dancers.[243]

Work

• When he was young and inexperienced, Hector Gray worked as a dancer for producer Walter Johnson. This was exhausting work, as no union existed to limit the number of rehearsal hours. At a rehearsal one day, Mr. Gray was so exhausted that he walked off the stage rather than dancing off as he should have. Mr. Johnson severely criticized him for it, and Mr. Gray replied, "Do better." Mr. Johnson then answered, "I shall." A few minutes later, the music of Mr. Gray's favorite dance started playing, and a just-promoted former member of the chorus stepped out and started dancing. Mr. Gray was fired.[244]

• Master choreographer George Balanchine worked much with ballerina Suzanne Farrell. Another ballerina, Maria Tallchief, understood why when she gave a dance class that Ms. Farrell attended. Ms. Farrell was a little unsteady while holding her leg out to the side, so Ms. Tallchief corrected her, saying that she could steady herself by raising her leg higher. Ms. Farrell immediately raised her leg — almost above her head. Ms. Tallchief was astonished: "Oh, my goodness .... Now I see. This is the material George wants to work with."[245]

• When Misha Baryshnikov defected from the USSR in 1974, Rudolf Nureyev, who had defected earlier, took him to dinner. Mr. Baryshnikov was 10 years younger than Mr. Nureyev, who pointed to him and said, "Now I will have to work 10 times as hard to keep up with new competition." Mr. Nureyev was asked, "How can you work harder? No one works harder than you!" He narrowed his eyes and said, "Watch me!"[246]

• Georges Skibine was dancing for Colonel de Basil's company when its financing was cut off due to World War II. While the company was on tour in Cuba, Colonel de Basil announced that he was cutting each dancer's salary in half. Rather than take the pay cut, Mr. Skibine left the company and took a job as a cook in Cuba. Eventually, he made his way to New York and later even danced for Colonel de Basil again. [247]

• Krissie Illing made a living in street theater — something she obviously was very proud of. She was trained in both dance and mime, and she worked with Mark Britton in the duo Nickelodeon. Ms. Illing once said, "It's taken me 29 years to prove to my father that I can work and earn a living like this. He used to say, 'Why don't you take an office job and keep your dancing as a hobby?'"[248]

• Dancers work extremely hard, making their day of rest extremely important. Karen Kain and Frank Augustyn were once offered a lot of money to dance on a Canadian television program on their day of rest, but they turned the money down. Ms. Kain explained, "We didn't want to dance on our rest day — it might have led to a poor performance later that week."[249]

• The Shah of Persia was extremely wealthy and had lots of dancing girls. Once, he observed a lot of people dancing at a society ball in Paris, and he asked, "Can't these people hire someone to do this for them?" [250]

Appendix A: Bibliography

Adler, Bill. *Fred Astaire: A Wonderful Life.* New York: Carroll & Graf Publishers, Inc., 1987.

Aflaki, Shams al-Din Ahmad. *Legends of the Sufis: Selected Anecdotes from the Work Entitled The Acts of the Adepts by Shemsu-'D-Din Ahmed, El Eflaki.* London: Theosophical Publishing House, 1976.

Algeranoff, H. *My Years With Pavlova.* London: William Heinemann, Ltd., 1957.

Anthony, Gordon. *A Camera at the Ballet: Pioneer Dancers of the Royal Ballet.* Newton Abbot, Devon: David & Charles, Limited, 1975.

Arnold, Sandra Martin. *Alicia Alonso: First Lady of the Ballet.* New York: Walker and Company, 1993.

Atkinson, Margaret F., and May Hillman. *Dancers of the Ballet.* New York: Alfred A. Knopf, 1955.

Augustyn, Frank, and Shelley Tanaka. *Footnotes: Dancing the World's Best-Loved Ballets.* Brookfield, CT: The Millbrook Press, 2001.

Baer, Nancy Van Norman. *Bronislava Nijinska: A Dancer's Legacy.* San Francisco, CA: Fine Arts Museums of San Francisco, 1986.

Banks, Morwenna, and Amanda Swift. *The Joke's on Us: Women in Comedy from Music Hall to the Present Day.* London: Pandora Press, 1987.

Barber, David W. *Tutus, Tights, and Tiptoes: Ballet History as It Ought to be Taught.* Toronto, Canada: Sound and Vision, 2000.

Barber, David W. *When the Fat Lady Sings: Opera History as It Ought to be Taught.* Toronto, Canada: Sound and Vision, 1990.

Barnes, Clive. *Inside American Ballet Theatre.* New York: Hawthorn Books, 1977.

Beaumont, Cyril W. *Vaslav Nijinsky.* New York: Haskell House Publishers, 1974.

Bing, Sir Rudolf. *5000 Nights at the Opera.* Garden City, NY: Doubleday and Company, Inc., 1972.

Bland, Alexander. *Fonteyn and Nureyev.* New York: Times Books, 1979.

Brubach, Holly. *Ten Dancers.* Photographs by Pierre Petitjean. New York: William Morrow and Company, Inc., 1982.

Clark, Mary Otis. *Leonide Massine: The Prodigal's Return to San Francisco in 1977.* Walnut Creek, CA: M.O. Clark, 1980.

Clarke, Mary. *Antoinette Sibley.* Photographs by Leslie E. Spatt. Introduction by Sir Frederick Ashton. London: Dance Books, 1981.

Crickmay, Anthony, photographer. *A Portrait of the Royal Theater.* London: Michael O'Mara Books, Limited, 1988.

Cruz, Barbara C. *Rubén Blades: Salsa Singer and Social Activist*. Springfield, NJ: Enslow Publications, Inc., 1997.

Danilova, Alexandra. *Choura: The Memoirs of Alexandra Danilova*. New York: Alfred A. Knopf, 1986.

Danneskiold, Jim; Mary Anne Santos Newhall; Julie Adams Strandberg, editors. *Dancing Rebels: Editor's Second Draft*. Providence, RI: American Dance Legacy Institute, 2005. Deborah Friedes, Mary Anne Santos Newhall, Kyle Shepard, researchers/writers; Mary Anne Santos Newhall, research consultant and mentor.

de Mille, Agnes. *Portrait Gallery*. Boston, MA: Houghton Mifflin Company, 1990.

Deedy, John. *A Book of Catholic Anecdotes*. Allen, TX: Thomas More, 1997.

dePaola, Tomie. *Things Will NEVER Be the Same*. New York: G.P. Putnam's Sons, 2003.

Dolin, Anton. *Alicia Markova: Her Life and Art*. New York: Hermitage House, 1953.

Duncan, Isadora. *Isadora Speaks*. Edited and with an introduction by Franklin Rosemont. San Francisco, CA: City Lights Books, 1981.

Editors of Dance Magazine, with text by Gloria Manor. *The Gospel According to Dance*. New York: St. Martin's Press, 1980.

Farrell, Suzanne. *Holding On to the Air*. New York: Summit Books, 1990.

Feinberg, Morris "Moe." *Larry: The Stooge in the Middle*. San Francisco, CA: Last Gasp of San Francisco, 1984.

Finck, Henry T. *Musical Laughs*. New York: Funk & Wagnalls Company, 1924.

Fisher, Hugh. *Alicia Markova*. New York: The Macmillan Company, 1954.

Fletcher, Lynne Yamaguchi. *The First Gay Pope and Other Records*. Boston, MA: Alyson Publications, Inc., 1992.

Fonteyn, Margot. *Autobiography*. New York: Alfred A. Knopf, 1976.

Fonteyn, Margot, presenter. *Pavlova: Portrait of a Dancer*. New York: Viking Penguin, Inc., 1984.

Ford, Carin T. *Legends of American Dance and Choreography*. Berkeley Heights, NJ: Enslow Publications, Inc., 2000.

Franklin, Joe. *Joe Franklin's Encyclopedia of Comedians*. Secaucus, NJ: The Citadel Press, 1979.

Franks, A.H., editor. *Pavlova: A Collection of Memoirs*. New York: Da Capo Press, Inc., 1956.

Freedman, Russell. *Martha Graham: A Dancer's Life*. New York: Clarion Books, 1998.

Freeman, Gillian, and Edward Thorpe. *Ballet Genius*. London: Equation, 1988.

Gale, Joseph. *Behind Barres: The Mystique of Masterly Teaching.* New York: Dance Horizons, 1980.

Garden, Mary, and Louis Biancolli. *Mary Garden's Story.* New York: Simon and Schuster, Inc., 1951.

Garfunkel, Trudy. *Letter to the World: The Life and Dances of Martha Graham.* Boston, MA: Little, Brown and Company, 1995.

Garfunkel, Trudy. *On Wings of Joy: The Story of Ballet from the 16th Century to Today.* Boston, MA: Little, Brown and Company, 1994.

Gershick, Zsa Zsa. *Gay Old Girls.* Los Angeles, CA: Alyson Books, 1998.

Giles, Sarah. *Fred Astaire: His Friends Talk.* New York: Doubleday, 1988.

Glassman, Bruce. *Mikhail Baryshnikov: Dance Genius.* Woodbridge, CT: Blackbirch Press, Inc., 2001.

Glover, Savion, and Bruce Weber. *Savion! My Life in Tap.* New York: William Morrow and Company, Inc., 2000.

Goh, Chan Hon. *Beyond the Dance: A Ballerina's Life.* With Cary Fagan. Toronto, Ontario, Canada: Tundra Books, 2002.

Gonzales, Doreen. *AIDS: Ten Stories of Courage.* Springfield, NJ: Enslow Publications, Inc., 1996.

Goodman, Jack, and Albert Rice. *I Wish I'd Said That!* New York: Simon and Schuster, 1935.

Gordon, Mel. *The Seven Addictions and Five Professions of Anita Berber: Weimar Berlin's Priestess of Depravity.* Los Angeles, CA: Feral House, 2006.

Gottlieb, Robert. *George Balanchine: The Ballet Maker.* New York: HarperCollins Publishers, Inc., 2004.

Gourley, Catherine. *Who is Maria Tallchief?* New York: Grosset and Dunlap, 2002.

Govenar, Alan, collector and editor. *Stompin' at the Savoy: The Story of Norma Miller.* Cambridge, MA: Candlewick Press, 2006.

Gray, Hector. *An Actor Looks Back.* Hobart Tasmania: Cat and Fiddle Press, 1973.

Gregory, Cynthia. *Cynthia Gregory Dances Swan Lake.* New York: Simon and Schuster, Inc., 1990.

Gregory, John, editor. *Heritage of a Ballet Master: Nicolas Legat.* London: Dance Books, Ltd., 1978.

Greskovic, Robert. *Ballet 101.* New York: Hyperion, 1998.

Grody, Svetlana McLee, and Dorothy Daniels Lister. *Conversations With Choreographers.* Portsmouth, NH: Heinemann, 1996.

Gruen, John. *People Who Dance.* Pennington, NJ: Princeton Book Company, 1988.

Hammond, Joan. *A Voice, A Life*. London: Victor Gollancz, Ltd., 1970.

Harris, Margaret Haile, *Loïe Fuller: Magician of Light*. Richmond, VA: The Virginia Museum, 1979.

Hasday, Judy L. *Agnes de Mille*. Philadelphia, PA: Chelsea House Publishers, 2004.

Haskell, Arnold L. *Ballet Vignettes*. Edinburgh, Scotland: The Albyn Press, 1948.

Haskins, Jim, and N.R. Mitgang. *Mr. Bojangles: The Story of Bill Robinson*. New York: William Morrow and Company, Inc., 1988.

Hewlett-Davies, Barry, editor and compiler. *A Night at the Opera*. New York: St. Martin's Press, 1980.

Hodgson, Moira. *Quintet: Five American Dance Companies*. Photographs by Thomas Victor. New York: William Morrow and Company, Inc., 1976.

Horosko, Marian. *May O'Donnell: Modern Dance Pioneer*. Gainesville, FL: University Press of Florida, 2005.

Huckenpahler, Victoria. *Ballerina: A Biography of Violette Verdy*. New York: Marcel Dekker, Inc., 1978.

Hurok, S. *S. Hurok Presents: A Memoir of the Dance World*. New York: Hermitage House, 1953.

Joiner, Beth. *Gotta Dance!* New York: Vantage Press, 1985.

Kahn, Albert E. *Days With Ulanova*. New York: Simon and Schuster, 1962.

Karkar, Jack and Waltraud, compilers and editors. *... And They Danced On*. Wausau, WI: Aardvark Enterprises, 1989.

Katkov, Norman. *The Fabulous Fanny*. New York: Alfred A. Knopf, 1953.

Kistler, Darci. *Ballerina: My Story*. With Alicia Kistler. New York: Pocket Books, Inc., 1993.

Klosty, James, editor and photographer. *Merce Cunningham*. New York: Saturday Review Press/E.P. Dutton and Co., Inc., 1975.

Kristy, Davida. *George Balanchine: American Ballet Master*. Minneapolis, MN: Lerner Publications Company, 1996.

Ladré, Illaria Obidenna. *Illaria Obidenna Ladré: Memoirs of a Child of Theatre Street*. With Nancy Whyte. Seattle, WA: The Author, 1988.

Lang, Paul. *Maria Tallchief: Native American Ballerina*. Springfield, NJ: Enslow Publications, Inc., 1997.

Laskas, Jeanne Marie. *We Remember: Women Born at the Turn of the Century Tell the Stories of Their Lives*. Photographs by Lynn Johnson. New York: William Morrow and Company, 1999.

Legat, Nicolas. *Ballet Russe: Memoirs of Nicolas Legat*. Translated by Sir Paul Dukes. London: Methuen & Co., Ltd., 1939.

Levine, Ellen. *Anna Pavlova: Genius of the Dance*. New York: Scholastic, Inc., 1995.

Lewis-Ferguson, Julinda. *Alvin Ailey, Jr.* New York: Walker and Company, 1994.

Little, Jean. *Little by Little: A Writer's Education*. Ontario, Canada: Viking Kestrel, 1987.

Long, Rod. *Belly Laughs*. Renton, WI: Talion Publishing, 1999.

Makarova, Natalia. *A Dance Autobiography*. Edited by Gennady Smakov. New York: Alfred A Knopf, Inc., 1979.

Markova, Alicia. *Giselle and Me*. New York: The Vanguard Press, Inc., 1960.

Markova, Alicia. *Markova Remembers*. Boston, MA: Little, Brown and Company, 1986.

Martins, Peter. *Far From Denmark*. With Robert Cornfield. Boston, MA: Little, Brown and Company, 1982.

Marx, Samuel. *Broadway Portraits*. New York: Donald Flamm, Inc., 1929.

Massine, Léonide. *My Life in Ballet*. Edited by Phyllis Hartnoll and Robert Rubens. London: Macmillan and Co., Ltd., 1968.

Matthews, Denis. *In Pursuit of Music*. London: Victor Gollancz, Ltd., 1966.

Maybarduk, Linda. *The Dancer Who Flew: A Memoir of Rudolf Nureyev*. Toronto, Ontario, Canada: Tundra Books, 1999.

Mercredi, Morningstar. *Fort Chipewyan Homecoming: A Journey to Native Canada*. Minneapolis, MN: Lerner Publications Company, 1997.

Miller, Claudia. *Shannon Miller: My Child, My Hero*. Norman, OK: University of Oklahoma Press, 1999.

Miller, John. *Ralph Richardson: The Authorized Biography*. London: Sidgwick and Jackson, 1995.

Miller, Norma. *Swingin' at the Savoy*. With Evette Jensen. Philadelphia, PA: Temple University Press, 1996.

Montague, Sarah. *Pas de Deux: Great Partnerships in Dance*. New York: Universe Books, 1981.

Monteux, Doris G. *It's All in the Music*. New York: Farrar, Straus and Giroux, 1965.

Moore, Grace. *You're Only Human Once*. Garden City, NY: Doubleday, Doran and Co., Inc., 1944.

Neale, Wendy. *Ballet Life Behind the Scenes*. New York: Crown Publishers, Inc., 1982.

Nemenschousky, Léon. *A Day with Marjorie Tallchief and Georges Skibine*. London: Cassell and Company, Ltd., 1960.

Nemenschousky, Léon. *A Day With Yvette Chauviré*. London: Cassell & Company, Ltd., 1960.

Newman, Barbara, and Leslie E. Spatt. *Swan Lake*. London: Dance Books, 1983.

Norkin, Sam. *Drawings, Stories: Theater, Opera, Ballet, Movies*. Portsmouth, NH: Heinemann, 1994.

Nureyev, Rudolf. *Nureyev: An Autobiography*. New York: E.P. Dutton and Co., Inc., 1963.

O'Connor, Barbara. *Barefoot Dancer: The Story of Isadora Duncan*. Minneapolis, MN: Carolrhoda Books, Inc., 1994.

O'Connor, Barbara. *Katherine Dunham: Pioneer of Black Dance*. Minneapolis, MN: Carolrhoda Books, Inc., 2000.

Patelson, Alice. *Portrait of a Dancer, Memories of Balanchine: An Autobiography*. New York: Vantage Press, 1995.

Péres, Louis. *Cynthia Gregory*. Brooklyn, NY: Dance Horizons, 1975.

Perry, Joel. *Funny That Way: Adventures in Fabulousness*. Los Angeles, CA: Alyson Books, 2001.

Peters, Russell M. *Clambake: A Wampanoag Tradition*. Minneapolis, MN: Lerner Publications Company, 1992.

Pollack, Barbara, and Charles Humphrey Woodford. *Dance is a Moment: A Portrait of José Limón in Words and Pictures*. Pennington, NJ: Princeton Book Company, Publishers, 1993.

Pratt, Paula Bryant. *Martha Graham*. San Diego, CA: Lucent Books, 1995.

Riley, Gail Blasser. *Wah Ming Chang: Artist and Master of Special Effects*. Springfield, NJ: Enslow Publications, Inc., 1995.

Robinson, Simon. *A Year With Rudolf Nureyev*. With Derek Robinson. London: Robert Hale, Limited, 1997.

Rodriguez-Hunter, Suzanne. *Found Meals of the Lost Generation*. Boston, MA: Faber and Faber, 1994.

Rogosin, Elinor. *The Dance Makers: Conversations with American Choreographers*. New York: Walker and Company, 1980.

Roseman, Janet Lynn. *Dance Masters: Interviews with Legends of Dance*. New York: Routledge, 2001.

Rosen, Lillie F. *Jacques d'Amboise*. Photographs by Martha Swope. Brooklyn, NY: Dance Horizons, 1975.

Savage, Richard Temple. *A Voice from the Pit*. Newton Abbot; North Pomfret, VT: David & Charles, 1988.

Shawn, Ted. *One Thousand and One Night Stands*. With Gray Poole. New York: Da Capo Press, Inc., 1979.

Silverman, Stephen M. *Funny Ladies: The Women Who Make Us Laugh*. New York: Harry N. Abrams, Inc., 1999.

Smith, H. Allen. *Buskin' With H. Allen Smith*. New York: Trident Press, 1968.

Sorel, Nancy Caldwell, and Edward Sorel. *First Encounters: A Book of Memorable Meetings*. New York: Alfred A. Knopf, 1994.

Speaker-Yuan, Margaret. *Agnes de Mille*. New York: Chelsea House Publishers, 1990.

Street, David. *Karen Kain: Lady of Dance*. Text by David Mason. Toronto, Canada: McGraw-Hill Ryerson, Limited, 1978.

Stier, Theodore. *With Pavlova Around the World*. London: Hurst & Blackett, Ltd., 1927.

Story, Rosalyn M. *And So I Sing: African-American Divas of Opera and Concert*. New York: Warner Books, 1990.

Stuart, Andrea. *Showgirls*. London: Jonathan Cape, 1996.

Szilard, Paul. *Under My Wings: My Life as an Impresario*. New York: Limelight Editions, 2002.

Tallchief, Maria. *Maria Tallchief: America's Prima Ballerina*. With Larry Kaplan. New York: Henry Holt and Company, 1997.

Teachout, Terry. *All in the Dances: A Brief Life of George Balanchine*. New York: Harcourt, Inc., 2004.

Terry, Walter. *Star Performance: The Story of the World's Great Ballerinas*. Garden City, NY: Doubleday & Co., Inc., 1954.

Terry, Walter. *Ted Shawn: Father of American Dance*. New York: The Dial Press, 1976.

Tharp, Twyla. *Push Comes to Shove*. New York: Bantam Books, 1992.

Thomas, Kurt, and Kent Hannon. *Kurt Thomas on Gymnastics*. New York: Simon and Schuster, 1980.

Tracy, Robert, and Sharon DeLano. *Balanchine's Ballerinas: Conversations with the Muses*. New York: Linden Press/Simon and Schuster, 1983.

Villella, Edward. *Prodigal Son: Dancing for Balanchine in a World of Pain and Magic*. With Larry Kaplan. New York: Simon & Schuster, Inc., 1992.

Waters, John. *Crackpot: The Obsessions of John Waters*. New York: Vintage Books, 1987.

Wheatcroft, Andrew, compiler. *Dolin: Friends and Memories*. London and Henley: Routledge & Kegan Paul, 1982.

Woolf, Vicki. *Dancing in the Vortex: The Story of Ida Rubinstein*. Australia: Harwood Academic Publishers, 2000.

Zolotow, Maurice. *No People Like Show People*. New York: Random House, 1951.

Zoritch, George. *Ballet Mystique: Behind the Glamour of the Ballet Russe*. Mountain View, CA: Cynara Editions, 2000.

Appendix B: About the Author

It was a dark and stormy night. Suddenly a cry rang out, and on a hot summer night in 1954, Josephine, wife of Carl Bruce, gave birth to a boy — me. Unfortunately, this young married couple allowed Reuben Saturday, Josephine's brother, to name their first-born. Reuben, aka "The Joker," decided that Bruce was a nice name, so he decided to name me Bruce Bruce. I have gone by my middle name — David — ever since.

Being named Bruce David Bruce hasn't been all bad. Bank tellers remember me very quickly, so I don't often have to show an ID. It can be fun in charades, also. When I was a counselor as a teenager at Camp Echoing Hills in Warsaw, Ohio, a fellow counselor gave the signs for "sounds like" and "two words," then she pointed to a bruise on her leg twice. Bruise Bruise? Oh yeah, Bruce Bruce is the answer!

Uncle Reuben, by the way, gave me a haircut when I was in kindergarten. He cut my hair short and shaved a small bald spot on the back of my head. My mother wouldn't let me go to school until the bald spot grew out again.

Of all my brothers and sisters (six in all), I am the only transplant to Athens, Ohio. I was born in Newark, Ohio, and have lived all around Southeastern Ohio. However, I moved to Athens to go to Ohio University and have never left.

At Ohio U, I never could make up my mind whether to major in English or Philosophy, so I got a bachelor's degree with a double major in both areas, then I added a Master of Arts degree in English and a Master of Arts degree in Philosophy. Yes, I have my MAMA degree.

Currently, and for a long time to come (I eat fruits and veggies), I am spending my retirement writing books such as *Nadia Comaneci: Perfect 10*, *The Funniest People in Comedy*, *Homer's* Iliad: *A Retelling in Prose*, and *William Shakespeare's* Hamlet: *A Retelling in Prose*.

If all goes well, I will publish one or two books a year for the rest of my life. (On the other hand, a good way to make God laugh is to tell Her your plans.)

By the way, my sister Brenda Kennedy writes romances such as *A New Beginning* and *Shattered Dreams*.

Appendix C: Some Books by David Bruce

Anecdote Collections

250 Anecdotes About Opera
250 Anecdotes About Religion
250 Anecdotes About Religion: Volume 2
250 Music Anecdotes
Be a Work of Art: 250 Anecdotes and Stories
The Coolest People in Art: 250 Anecdotes
The Coolest People in the Arts: 250 Anecdotes
The Coolest People in Books: 250 Anecdotes
The Coolest People in Comedy: 250 Anecdotes
Create, Then Take a Break: 250 Anecdotes
Don't Fear the Reaper: 250 Anecdotes
The Funniest People in Art: 250 Anecdotes
The Funniest People in Books: 250 Anecdotes
The Funniest People in Books, Volume 2: 250 Anecdotes
The Funniest People in Books, Volume 3: 250 Anecdotes
The Funniest People in Comedy: 250 Anecdotes
The Funniest People in Dance: 250 Anecdotes
The Funniest People in Families: 250 Anecdotes
The Funniest People in Families, Volume 2: 250 Anecdotes
The Funniest People in Families, Volume 3: 250 Anecdotes
The Funniest People in Families, Volume 4: 250 Anecdotes
The Funniest People in Families, Volume 5: 250 Anecdotes
The Funniest People in Families, Volume 6: 250 Anecdotes
The Funniest People in Movies: 250 Anecdotes
The Funniest People in Music: 250 Anecdotes
The Funniest People in Music, Volume 2: 250 Anecdotes
The Funniest People in Music, Volume 3: 250 Anecdotes
The Funniest People in Neighborhoods: 250 Anecdotes
The Funniest People in Relationships: 250 Anecdotes
The Funniest People in Sports: 250 Anecdotes
The Funniest People in Sports, Volume 2: 250 Anecdotes
The Funniest People in Television and Radio: 250 Anecdotes
The Funniest People in Theater: 250 Anecdotes

The Funniest People Who Live Life: 250 Anecdotes

The Funniest People Who Live Life, Volume 2: 250 Anecdotes

The Kindest People Who Do Good Deeds, Volume 1: 250 Anecdotes

The Kindest People Who Do Good Deeds, Volume 2: 250 Anecdotes

Maximum Cool: 250 Anecdotes

The Most Interesting People in Movies: 250 Anecdotes

The Most Interesting People in Politics and History: 250 Anecdotes

The Most Interesting People in Politics and History, Volume 2: 250 Anecdotes

The Most Interesting People in Politics and History, Volume 3: 250 Anecdotes

The Most Interesting People in Religion: 250 Anecdotes

The Most Interesting People in Sports: 250 Anecdotes

The Most Interesting People Who Live Life: 250 Anecdotes

The Most Interesting People Who Live Life, Volume 2: 250 Anecdotes

Reality is Fabulous: 250 Anecdotes and Stories

Resist Psychic Death: 250 Anecdotes

Seize the Day: 250 Anecdotes and Stories

[1] Source: Barbara C. Cruz, *Rubén Blades: Salsa Singer and Social Activist*, p. 60.

[2] Source: Julinda Lewis-Ferguson, *Alvin Ailey, Jr.*, pp. 65-67.

[3] Source: Alice Patelson, *Portrait of a Dancer, Memories of Balanchine: An Autobiography*, pp. 1-2.

[4] Source: Rod Long, *Belly Laughs*, pp. 13ff.

[5] Source: Rudolf Nureyev, *Nureyev: An Autobiography*, pp. 33-34.

[6] Source: Barbara O'Connor, *Katherine Dunham: Pioneer of Black Dance*, p. 45.

[7] Source: Russell Freedman, *Martha Graham: A Dancer's Life*, pp. 33-35.

[8] Source: Norma Miller, *Swingin' at the Savoy*, pp. 87-88.

[9] Source: Clive Barnes, *Inside American Ballet Theatre*, p. 86.

[10] Source: Mel Gordon, *The Seven Addictions and Five Professions of Anita Berber*, pp. 112-113.

[11] Source: Barbara O'Connor, *Barefoot Dancer: The Story of Isadora Duncan*, p. 25.

[12] Source: Twyla Tharp, *Push Comes to Shove*, pp. 270-271.

[13] Source: Cyril W. Beaumont, *Vaslav Nijinsky*, p. 20.

[14] Source: Victoria Huckenpahler, *Ballerina: A Biography of Violette Verdy*, p. 77.

[15] Source: Nancy Caldwell Sorel and Edward Sorel, *First Encounters*, p. 13.

[16] Source: Elinor Rogosin, *The Dance Makers: Conversations with American Choreographers*, p. 70.

[17] Source: Jim Danneskiold, et al., editors, *Dancing Rebels: Editor's Second Draft*, p. 63.

[18] Source: Davida Kristy, *George Balanchine: American Ballet Master*, p. 28.

[19] Source: George Zoritch, *Ballet Mystique: Behind the Glamour of the Ballet Russe*, p. 143.

[20] Source: Alice Patelson, *Portrait of a Dancer, Memories of Balanchine: An Autobiography*, p. 65.

[21] Source: Illaria Obidenna Ladré, *Illaria Obidenna Ladré: Memoirs of a Child of Theatre Street*, p. 8.

[22] Source: The documentary *Martha Graham: The Dancer Revealed*.

[23] Source: Holly Brubach, *Ten Dancers*, p. 145.

[24] Source: Janet Lynn Roseman, *Dance Masters: Interviews with Legends of Dance*, pp. 137, 151-152.

[25] Source: Margot Fonteyn, presenter, *Pavlova: Portrait of a Dancer*, p. 120.

[26] Source: Illaria Obidenna Ladré, *Illaria Obidenna Ladré: Memoirs of a Child of Theatre Street*, p. 39.

[27] Source: Margot Fonteyn, *Autobiography*, p. 11.

[28] Source: Beth Joiner, *Gotta Dance!*, pp. x-xi.

[29] Source Isadora Duncan, *Isadora Speaks*, pp. 23-24, 27.

[30] Source: Albert E. Kahn, *Days With Ulanova*, pp. 20, 121.

[31] Source: Judy L. Hasday, *Agnes de Mille*, pp. 54-55.

[32] Source: Suzanne Rodriguez-Hunter, *Found Meals of the Lost Generation*, p. 139.

[33] Source: Jean Little, *Little by Little: A Writer's Education*, p. 183.

[34] Source: Tomie dePaola, *Things Will NEVER Be the Same*, pp. 38-39.

[35] Source: Claudia Miller, *Shannon Miller: My Child, My Hero*, p. 11.

[36] Source: Suzanne Farrell, *Holding On to the Air*, p. 32.

[37] Source: Doreen Gonzales, *AIDS: Ten Stories of Courage*, p. 59.

[38] Source: Alexander Bland, *Fonteyn and Nureyev*, p. 12.

[39] Source: Margot Fonteyn, presenter, *Pavlova: Portrait of a Dancer*, p. 17.

[40] Source: Catherine Gourley, *Who is Maria Tallchief?*, p. 97.

[41] Source: Robert Tracy and Sharon DeLano, *Balanchine's Ballerinas: Conversations with the Muses*, p. 45.

[42] Source: Sam Norkin, *Drawings, Stories*, p. 326.

[43] Source: Svetlana McLee Grody and Dorothy Daniels Lister, *Conversations With Choreographers*, p. 179.

[44] Source: Robert Gottlieb, *George Balanchine: The Ballet Maker*, p. 188.

[45] Source: Trudy Garfunkel, *On Wings of Joy*, pp. 94-96.

[46] Source: Cyril W. Beaumont, *Vaslav Nijinsky*, p. 18.

[47] Source: Robert Gottlieb, *George Balanchine: The Ballet Maker*, p. 181.

[48] Source: Léon Nemenschousky, *A Day with Marjorie Tallchief and Georges Skibine*, pp. 37, 40.

[49] Source: Anton Dolin, *Alicia Markova: Her Life and Art*, p. 196.

[50] Source: Rod Long, *Belly Laughs*, pp. 135-136.

[51] Source: Sarah Giles, *Fred Astaire: His Friends Talk*, p. 55.

[52] Source: Alicia Markova, *Markova Remembers*, p. 8.

[53] Source: Bruce Glassman, *Mikhail Baryshnikov: Dance Genius*, pp. 31-32.

[54] Source: Holly Brubach, *Ten Dancers*, p. 199.

[55] Source: Andrew Wheatcroft, compiler, *Dolin: Friends and Memories*, pages are unnumbered.

[56] Source: Trudy Garfunkel, *Letter to the World: The Life and Dances of Martha Graham*, pp. 31-32.

[57] Source: Agnes de Mille, *Portrait Gallery*, p. 28.

[58] Source: Barbara O'Connor, *Barefoot Dancer: The Story of Isadora Duncan*, pp. 19-20, 81.

[59] Source: Paula Bryant Pratt, *Martha Graham*, p. 36.

[60] Source: Nancy Van Norman Baer, *Bronislava Nijinska: A Dancer's Legacy*, p. 40.

[61] Source: Margaret Speaker-Yuan, *Agnes de Mille*, p. 72.

[62] Source: Walter Terry, *Ted Shawn: Father of American Dance*, pp. 112-113.

[63] Source: Elinor Rogosin, *The Dance Makers: Conversations with American Choreographers*, p. 111.

[64] Source: Léon Nemenschousky, *A Day With Yvette Chauviré*, p. 13.

[65] Source: James Klosty, editor and photographer, *Merce Cunningham*, p. 30.

[66] Source: Moira Hodgson, *Quintet: Five American Dance Companies*, p. 12.

[67] Source: Carin T. Ford, *Legends of American Dance and Choreography*, pp. 81-82.

[68] Source: Trudy Garfunkel, *On Wings of Joy*, p. 40.

[69] Source: Julinda Lewis-Ferguson, *Alvin Ailey, Jr.*, pp. 71-74.

[70] Source: Chan Hon Goh, *Beyond the Dance: A Ballerina's Life*, pp. 20, 49-50.

[71] Source: Robert Tracy and Sharon DeLano, *Balanchine's Ballerinas: Conversations with the Muses*, pp. 66-67.

[72] Source: Russell Freedman, *Martha Graham: A Dancer's Life*, p. 31.

[73] Source: Moira Hodgson, *Quintet: Five American Dance Companies*, p. 120.

[74] Source: Agnes de Mille, *Portrait Gallery*, pp. 52-53.

[75] Source: Edward Villella, *Prodigal Son: Dancing for Balanchine in a World of Pain and Magic*, p. 70.

[76] Source: Terry Teachout, *All in the Dances: A Brief Life of George Balanchine*, p. 54.

[77] Source: Beth Joiner, *Gotta Dance!*, pp. ix-x.

[78] Source: Victoria Huckenpahler, *Ballerina: A Biography of Violette Verdy*, p. v.

[79] Source: A.H. Franks, editor, *Pavlova: A Collection of Memoirs*, pp. 77-78.

[80] Source: Maria Tallchief, *Maria Tallchief: America's Prima Ballerina*, pp. 325-326.

[81] Source: Mary Clarke, *Antoinette Sibley*, p. 7.

[82] Source: Barbara Newman and Leslie E. Spatt, *Swan Lake*, pp. 9-10.

[83] Source: Janet Lynn Roseman, *Dance Masters: Interviews with Legends of Dance*, p. 36.

[84] Source: Terry Teachout, *All in the Dances: A Brief Life of George Balanchine*, p. 144.

[85] Source: Barbara Pollack and Charles Humphrey Woodford, *Dance is a Moment*, p. 20.

[86] Source: Anthony Crickmay, photographer, *A Portrait of the Royal Theater*, p. 54.

[87] Source: Joseph Gale, *Behind Barres*, pp. 3, 7.

[88] Source: Trudy Garfunkel, *Letter to the World: The Life and Dances of Martha Graham*, p. 22.

[89] Source: Judy L. Hasday, *Agnes de Mille*, p. 48.

[90] Source: John Gregory, editor, *Heritage of a Ballet Master*, p. 14.

[91] Source: Jim Haskins and N.R. Mitgang, *Mr. Bojangles*, p. 89.

[92] Source: Twyla Tharp, *Push Comes to Shove*, p. 78.

[93] Source: John Waters, *Crackpot: The Obsessions of John Waters*, p. 99.

[94] Source: Robert Greskovic, *Ballet 101*, p. 469.

[95] Source: Paul Szilard, *Under My Wings*, pp. 77-78.

[96] Source: Barry Hewlett-Davies, *A Night at the Opera*, p. 36.

[97] Source: Anton Dolin, *Alicia Markova: Her Life and Art*, p. 78.

[98] Source: James Klosty, editor and photographer, *Merce Cunningham*, p. 55.

[99] Source: Theodore Stier, *With Pavlova Around the World*, p. 111.

[100] Source: Rudolf Nureyev, *Nureyev: An Autobiography*, pp. 37-38.

[101] Source: Wendy Neale, *Ballet Life Behind the Scenes*, pp. 165-166.

[102] Source: Léonide Massine, *My Life in Ballet*, p. 218.

[103] Source: Henry T. Finck, *Musical Laughs*, pp. 65-66.

[104] Source: Lillie F. Rosen, *Jacques d'Amboise*, p. 3.

[105] Source: Suzanne Rodriguez-Hunter, *Found Meals of the Lost Generation*, p. 136.

[106] Source: Robert Greskovic, *Ballet 101*, p. xx.

[107] Source: Gillian Freeman and Edward Thorpe, *Ballet Genius*, p. 207.

[108] Source: H. Algeranoff, *My Years With Pavlova*, p. 95.

[109] Source: Joel Perry, *Funny That Way: Adventures in Fabulousness*, pp. 23, 93.

[110] Source: Zsa Zsa Gershick, *Gay Old Girls*, p. 50.

[111] Source: Lynne Yamaguchi Fletcher, *The First Gay Pope and Other Records*, p. 33.

[112] Source: Chan Hon Goh, *Beyond the Dance: A Ballerina's Life*, pp. 53-54, 131-133.

[113] Source: Davida Kristy, *George Balanchine: American Ballet Master*, pp. 44-45.

[114] Source: Sandra Martin Arnold, *Alicia Alonso: First Lady of the Ballet*, p. 4.

[115] Source: Margaret F. Atkinson and May Hillman, *Dancers of the Ballet*, p. 135.

[116] Source: Marian Horosko, *May O'Donnell: Modern Dance Pioneer*, p. 79.

[117] Source: Paul Lang, *Maria Tallchief: Native American Ballerina*, pp. 84-85.

[118] Source: The documentary *Dancing for Mr. B: Six Balanchine Ballerinas*.

[119] Source: Paul Lang, *Maria Tallchief: Native American Ballerina*, p. 83.

[120] Source: Samuel Marx, *Broadway Portraits*, p. 12.

[121] Source: Jim Danneskiold, et al., editors, *Dancing Rebels: Editor's Second Draft*, p. 62.

[122] Source: Nicolas Legat, *Ballet Russe*, pp. 36-37.

[123] Source: Walter Terry, *Star Performance*, p. 174.

[124] Source: Sandra Martin Arnold, *Alicia Alonso: First Lady of the Ballet*, pp. 1-3.

[125] Source: Margaret Speaker-Yuan, *Agnes de Mille*, pp. 100-101.

[126] Source: Ellen Levine, *Anna Pavlova: Genius of the Dance*, p. 108.

[127] Source: Barbara Newman and Leslie E. Spatt, *Swan Lake*, p. 63.

[128] Source: Simon Robinson, *A Year With Rudolf Nureyev*, p. 93.

[129] Source: Doris G. Monteux, *It's All in the Music*, pp. 82-83.

[130] Source: John Gregory, editor, *Heritage of a Ballet Master*, p. 23.

[131] Source: Jack and Waltraud Karkar, compilers and editors, *... And They Danced On*, p. 38.

[132] Source: Alexandra Danilova, *Choura*, p. 151.

[133] Source: Darci Kistler, *Ballerina: My Story*, p. 42.

[134] Source: David W. Barber, *Tutus, Tights, and Tiptoes: Ballet History as It Ought to be Taught*, p. 44.

[135] Source: S. Hurok, *S. Hurok Presents*, p. 88.

[136] Source: Personal anecdote.

[137] Source: Kurt Thomas and Kent Hannon, *Kurt Thomas on Gymnastics*, p. 48.

[138] Source: Margaret Haile Harris, *Loïe Fuller: Magician of Light*, p. 15.

[139] Source: S. Hurok, *S. Hurok Presents*, pp. 253-254.

[140] Source: Joan Hammond, *A Voice, A Life*, pp. 217-218.

[141] Source: Peter Martins, *Far From Denmark*, p. 21.

[142] Source: Suzanne Farrell, *Holding On to the Air*, p. 269.

[143] Source: Darci Kistler, *Ballerina: My Story*, p. 81.

[144] Source: Margot Fonteyn, *Autobiography*, p. 60.

[145] Source: Morris "Moe" Feinberg, *Larry: The Stooge in the Middle*, p. 140.

[146] Source: Bill Adler, *Fred Astaire: A Wonderful Life*, pp. 134-135.

[147] Source: Wendy Neale, *Ballet Life Behind the Scenes*, pp. 108-109.

[148] Source: Linda Maybarduk, *The Dancer Who Flew*, p. 93.

[149] Source: Stephen M. Silverman, *Funny Ladies*, p. 121.

[150] Source: Sarah Montague, *Pas de Deux*, p. 9.

[151] Source: Richard Temple Savage, *A Voice from the Pit*, p. 110.

[152] Source: Theodore Stier, *With Pavlova Around the World*, pp. 49-50. This anecdote has been told about many people in the arts; however, Theodore Stier — Ms. Pavlova's music director — says that he has personal knowledge that it happened to Ms. Pavlova.

[153] Source: John Gruen, *People Who Dance*, p. 154.

[154] Source: Vicki Woolf, *Dancing in the Vortex: The Story of Ida Rubinstein*, pp. 103-104.

[155] Source: Ted Shawn, *One Thousand and One Night Stands*, p. 187.

[156] Source: Andrea Stuart, *Showgirls*, p. 31.

[157] Source: David W. Barber, *When the Fat Lady Sings*, p. 130.

[158] Source: Samuel Marx, *Broadway Portraits*, p. 31.

[159] Source: Norma Miller, *Swingin' at the Savoy*, p. 19.

[160] Source: Margaret F. Atkinson and May Hillman, *Dancers of the Ballet*, p. 42.

[161] Source: Alicia Markova, *Markova Remembers*, p. 87.

[162] Source: Jeanne Marie Laskas, *We Remember*, pp. 8, 10.

[163] Source: Natalia Makarova, *A Dance Autobiography*, p. 80.

[164] Source: Sarah Giles, *Fred Astaire: His Friends Talk*, p. 8.

[165] Source: Bill Adler, *Fred Astaire: A Wonderful Life*, pp. 154-155.

[166] Source: Savion Glover and Bruce Weber, *Savion! My Life in Tap*, p. 40.

[167] Source: Edward Villella, *Prodigal Son: Dancing for Balanchine in a World of Pain and Magic*, p. 64.

[168] Source: Alexandra Danilova, *Choura*, p. 52.

[169] Source: Margaret Haile Harris, *Loïe Fuller: Magician of Light*, p. 25.

[170] Source: Russell M. Peters, *Clambake: A Wampanoag Tradition*, p. 38.

[171] Source: Morningstar Mercredi, *Fort Chipewyan Homecoming: A Journey to Native Canada*, p. 40.

[172] Source: Nancy Van Norman Baer, *Bronislava Nijinska: A Dancer's Legacy*, p. 39.

[173] Source: Editors of *Dance Magazine*, with text by Gloria Manor, *The Gospel According to Dance*, pp. 64, 72, 114.

[174] Source: Vicki Woolf, *Dancing in the Vortex: The Story of Ida Rubinstein*, pp. 17, 30.

[175] Source: Frank Augustyn and Shelley Tanaka, *Footnotes: Dancing the World's Best-Loved Ballets*, p. 13.

[176] Source: Mary Otis Clark, *Leonide Massine: The Prodigal's Return to San Francisco in 1977*, p. 35.

[177] Source: Barbara Pollack and Charles Humphrey Woodford, *Dance is a Moment*, p. 85.

[178] Source: Frank Augustyn and Shelley Tanaka, *Footnotes: Dancing the World's Best-Loved Ballets*, p. 89.

[179] Source: Gordon Anthony, *A Camera at the Ballet*, p. 6.

[180] Source: David Street, *Karen Kain: Lady of Dance*, p. 16.

[181] Source: John Miller, *Ralph Richardson*, p. 206.

[182] Source: Rosalyn M. Story, *And So I Sing: African-American Divas of Opera and Concert*, pp. 53-54.

[183] Source: Jim Haskins and N.R. Mitgang, *Mr. Bojangles*, p. 22.

[184] Source: Gail Blasser Riley, *Wah Ming Chang: Artist and Master of Special Effects*, p. 29.

[185] Source: Barbara O'Connor, *Katherine Dunham: Pioneer of Black Dance*, pp. 59-60.

[186] Source: Sir Rudolf Bing, *5000 Nights at the Opera*, p. 253.

[187] Source: Alan Govenar, collector and editor, *Stompin' at the Savoy: The Story of Norma Miller*, p. 38.

[188] Source: Norman Katkov, *Fabulous Fanny*, pp. 38, 47-48.

[189] Source: Walter Terry, *Ted Shawn: Father of American Dance*, pp. 153-154.

[190] Source: George Zoritch, *Ballet Mystique: Behind the Glamour of the Ballet Russe*, pp. 241-242.

[191] Source: Cynthia Gregory, *Cynthia Gregory Dances Swan Lake*, p. 22.

[192] Source: Editors of *Dance Magazine*, with text by Gloria Manor, *The Gospel According to Dance*, pp. 102, 104.

[193] Source: Ellen Levine, *Anna Pavlova: Genius of the Dance*, p. 86.

[194] Source: Sarah Montague, *Pas de Deux*, p. 38.

[195] Source: Léonide Massine, *My Life in Ballet*, p. 156.

[196] Source: Léon Nemenschousky, *A Day With Yvette Chauviré*, p. 24.

[197] Source: Alicia Markova, *Giselle and Me*, p. 52.

[198] Source: Hugh Fisher, *Alicia Markova*, p. 30.

[199] Source: John Gruen, *People Who Dance*, p. 54.

[200] Source: Mary Otis Clark, *Leonide Massine: The Prodigal's Return to San Francisco in 1977*, p. 17.

[201] Source: Peter Martins, *Far From Denmark*, pp. 30, 37-39.

[202] Source: A.H. Franks, editor, *Pavlova: A Collection of Memoirs*, pp. 78-79.

[203] Source: Mary Garden and Louis Biancolli, *Mary Garden's Story*, pp. 172-173.

[204] Source: Rusty E. Frank, *Tap!*, p. 142.

[205] Source: Andrew Wheatcroft, compiler, *Dolin: Friends and Memories*, pages are unnumbered.

[206] Source: Carin T. Ford, *Legends of American Dance and Choreography*, pp. 4-5, 23.

[207] Source: Natalia Makarova, *A Dance Autobiography*, p. 151.

[208] Source: Nicolas Legat, *Ballet Russe*, p. 59.

[209] Source: Shams al-Din Ahmad Aflaki, *Legends of the Sufis*, pp. 80-81.

[210] Source: John Deedy, *A Book of Catholic Anecdotes*, p. 90. (Original source: Michael T. Farrell, *National Catholic Reporter*, 15 December 1995.)

[211] Source: Mary Clarke, *Antoinette Sibley*, p. 6.

[212] Source: Albert E. Kahn, *Days With Ulanova*, p. 34.

[213] Source: Grace Moore, *You're Only Human Once*, p. 71.

[214] Source: Paula Bryant Pratt, *Martha Graham*, p. 96.

[215] Source: Doreen Gonzales, *AIDS: Ten Stories of Courage*, p. 64.

[216] Source: Walter Terry, *Star Performance*, p. 135.

[217] Source: David W. Barber, *Tutus, Tights, and Tiptoes: Ballet History as It Ought to be Taught*, p. 42.

[218] Source: Paul Szilard, *Under My Wings*, p. 81.

[219] Source: Svetlana McLee Grody and Dorothy Daniels Lister, *Conversations With Choreographers*, p. 152.

[220] Source: Ted Shawn, *One Thousand and One Night Stands*, p. 237.

[221] Source: Gordon Anthony, *A Camera at the Ballet*, p. 30.

[222] Source: Jack Goodman and Albert Rice, *I Wish I'd Said That!*, pp. 86, 88.

[223] Source: Louis Péres, *Cynthia Gregory*, p. 4.

[224] Source: Alexander Bland, *Fonteyn and Nureyev*, p. 85.

[225] Source: Rusty E. Frank, *Tap!*, pp. 47-48.

[226] Source: Gregory Hines, "Foreword" to Savion Glover and Bruce Weber's *Savion! My Life in Tap*, p. 7.

[227] Source: Joe Franklin, *Joe Franklin's Encyclopedia of Comedians*, p. 314.

[228] Source: Denis Matthews, *In Pursuit of Music*, pp. 71-72.

[229] Source: Richard Temple Savage, *A Voice from the Pit*, p. 48.

[230] Source: Sam Norkin, *Drawings, Stories*, p. 2.

[231] Source: Maurice Zolotow, *No People Like Show People*, p. 121.

[232] Source: John Miller, *Ralph Richardson*, p. 192.

[233] Source: Jack and Waltraud Karkar, compilers and editors, ... *And They Danced On*, p. 156.

[234] Source: H. Algeranoff, *My Years With Pavlova*, p. 84.

[235] Source: Marian Horosko, *May O'Donnell: Modern Dance Pioneer*, pp. 8-9.

[236] Source: Alicia Markova, *Giselle and Me*, p. 178.

[237] Source: Catherine Gourley, *Who is Maria Tallchief?*, p. 41.

[238] Source: Clive Barnes, *Inside American Ballet Theatre*, p. 83.

[239] Source: Andrea Stuart, *Showgirls*, p. 98.

[240] Source: Simon Robinson, *A Year With Rudolf Nureyev*, p. 133.

[241] Source: Gillian Freeman and Edward Thorpe, *Ballet Genius*, pp. 100, 102.

[242] Source: Joseph Gale, *Behind Barres*, p. 34.

[243] Source: Arnold L. Haskell, *Ballet Vignettes*, pp. 57, 65.

[244] Source: Hector Gray, *An Actor Looks Back*, pp. 10-11.

[245] Source: Maria Tallchief, *Maria Tallchief: America's Prima Ballerina*, pp. 311-312.

[246] Source: Linda Maybarduk, *The Dancer Who Flew*, pp. 144, 146.

[247] Source: Léon Nemenschousky, *A Day with Marjorie Tallchief and Georges Skibine*, p. 12.

[248] Source: Morwenna Banks and Amanda Swift, *The Joke's on Us*, p. 122.

[249] Source: David Street, *Karen Kain: Lady of Dance*, p. 12.

[250] Source: H. Allen Smith, *Buskin' With H. Allen Smith*, p. 139.